Henry W. Tucker

The English Church in Other Lands

Or, the spiritual expansion of England

Henry W. Tucker

The English Church in Other Lands
Or, the spiritual expansion of England

ISBN/EAN: 9783337000509

Printed in Europe, USA, Canada, Australia, Japan

Cover: Foto ©Lupo / pixelio.de

More available books at **www.hansebooks.com**

Epochs of Church History

EDITED BY THE

RÉV. MANDELL CREIGHTON, M.A.

THE

ENGLISH CHURCH IN OTHER LANDS

PRINTED BY
SPOTTISWOODE AND CO., NEW-STREET SQUARE
LONDON

THE ENGLISH CHURCH

IN OTHER LANDS

OR

THE SPIRITUAL EXPANSION OF ENGLAND

BY THE

REV. H. W. TUCKER, M.A.

PREBENDARY OF ST. PAUL'S

AUTHOR OF 'UNDER HIS BANNER,' 'MEMOIR OF THE LIFE AND EPISCOPATE OF
EDWARD FEILD, D.D.' 'MEMOIR OF THE LIFE AND EPISCOPATE OF
GEORGE AUGUSTUS SELWYN, D.D.' ETC.

LONDON
LONGMANS, GREEN, AND CO.
1886

'Now to the revolving sphere
We point and say, "No desert here,
No waste, so dark and lone,
But to the hour of sacrifice
Comes daily in its turn, and lies
In light before the Throne"'

PREFACE.

To compress into a small book the story of a work which has had the world for its field, and has been carried on for more than three centuries, I have found to be no easy task. While I have remembered the obligation of brevity, I have endeavoured to omit nothing that appeared to be essential to a clear understanding of the subject.

I have endeavoured to set forth what has been the missionary work, not only of the Anglican Communion, but of all the sections into which English Christianity is divided. I am glad to recognise and to hold in honour the zeal which prompts, and the practical wisdom which directs, the foreign missionary work of Nonconformist bodies, among whom the duty of taking a personal share in the spread of the Gospel seems to be recognised by all classes as a necessary part of their religious life.

To plant the Church of Christ in all lands is a work which demands not only persistent and undaunted zeal, but also practical and statesmanlike gifts of administration, to the suppression of the impetuous and selfish individualism which too often monopolises the name of Enthusiasm. It is a work which can be rightly carried out only by men who will be content to regard it as a whole, to legislate for it on system, to take a wide and equable survey of the condition of the whole field and the relative needs of all its parts, co-ordinating means and wants without favour, partiality, or prejudice.

The moral of the story will, I hope, unfold itself. It is that we, who are members of this Church or nation of England, are living in a time of unprecedented opportunities and of corresponding responsibilities, which are laid upon us as citizens and as Christians; for we are concerned with events that are rapidly changing the face of the world, and threaten to shift the centre of gravity of Christendom, so that at no distant time it may be found, neither at Constantinople nor at Rome, but at Canterbury.

Those who desire to study the subjects treated in this book in greater detail will find in 'Anderson's History of the Colonial Church' a storehouse of information in regard to the period of which those volumes speak. The late Archdeacon Hardwicke's 'Christ and other Masters,' Professor Max Müller's 'Chips from a German Workshop,' Canon Cook's 'Origins of Religion and Language,' and the small books on Non-Christian Religious Systems published by the Society for Promoting Christian Knowledge will tell all that it is necessary to know of the creeds which sway the consciences of hundreds of millions of our fellow-creatures. Miss Yonge's 'Pioneers and Founders;' the biographies of Bishops Middleton, Heber, Cotton, Milman, Venables, Feild, and Selwyn; of Livingstone, of Carey, of S. Francis Xavier, and others, while dealing with the work of individuals, will illustrate forcibly the general subject. 'Mission Work among the Indian Tribes of British Guiana,' by the late Rev. W. H. Brett; 'Personal Recollections of British Burmah,' by Bishop Titcomb; 'Sketches of Our Life at Sarawak,' by Mrs. McDougall; 'Twenty Years in Central Africa,' by Rev. H. Rowley, are the personal records of those who have themselves borne the burden of the foreign service of the Church. Lord Blachford, in a pamphlet entitled 'Some Account of the Legal Development of the Colonial Episcopate,' has given much valuable information on a matter, little understood, on which no one is more competent to write than the noble author himself, who for so long a period held a high position in the Colonial Office.

CONTENTS.

CHAPTER I.

GROWTH OF THE MISSIONARY SPIRIT.

PAGE

The Colonial Expansion of England—Its origin—Henry VIII.—Colonisation in the reign of Elizabeth—Other European nations and their Colonies—Colonies in time of James I.—of Charles I.—of Cromwell—of Charles II.—The East India Company—Colonisation in Eighteenth Century, and Nineteenth—The Spiritual Growth of the Colonies—Frobisher's Expedition—The Commonwealth and its care for religion—Council of foreign plantations—Prayer for all conditions of men—Boyle Lectures—Religious divisions—Dr. Bray and Dr. Blair—Dean Prideaux and East India Company—Origin of Society for Promoting Christian Knowledge, and Society for the Propagation of the Gospel—Danish Missions—Baptist and London Missionary Societies—Church Missionary Society—Summary—The Colonial Episcopate 1

CHAPTER II.

THE CHURCH IN THE UNITED STATES.

Early Settlement—John and Charles Wesley—Slavery—Persecution of Churchmen—Bishop Seabury—First Convention of American Church—Conversion of Indians—Growth of Church—Intercommunion 19

CHAPTER III.

THE CHURCH IN NEWFOUNDLAND, NOVA SCOTIA, QUEBEC, AND ONTARIO.

Early Settlements—The Acadians—Loyalist Refugees—First Colonial Bishop—Newfoundland and its Bishops—The Church in Canada—Bishop Stewart—Montreal—Upper Canada—Education in Canada—The Clergy Reserves . . 26

CHAPTER IV.

THE CHURCH IN NORTH-WEST CANADA.

The Hudson's Bay Company—Conversion of Indians—First English Bishop of Rupert's Land—The Canadian Pacific Railway—Immigration—Church growth—Isolation and hardship—Colonel Butler's description of the Mail Service in North-West Canada—Disappearance of Indians and Buffalos—British Columbia—Division of Diocese 39

CHAPTER V.

THE CHURCH IN THE WEST INDIES.

The Church Established and State-maintained—Bishop Butler on Slavery—Emancipation—The Episcopate—Disendowment—Self-help—British Honduras—General Codrington—His bequest to S. P. G.—Codrington College—Hayti and its Church 53

CHAPTER VI.

THE CHURCH IN SOUTH AMERICA.

British Guiana—Evangelistic Work among (1) Indian tribes; (2) Coolies—Rev. W. H. Brett—The Falkland Islands—Patagonia 60

CHAPTER VII.

THE CHURCH IN AUSTRALIA.

Loss of the American Colonies redressed by discovery of New Holland—Convict Settlements—Port Jackson—Ceremonies on laying foundations of Sydney—Free Immigrants—Archdeacon Broughton first Bishop of Australia—New Zealand and Tasmania visited—Growth of Australian Episcopate—Diocese of Newcastle—of Brisbane—of Grafton and Armidale—The Church and the Gold-diggers—Dioceses of Goulburn, Bathurst, Riverina, Melbourne, Ballaarat, Adelaide, Perth, Tasmania, North Queensland — Bishop Barry — Aborigines — Their treatment — Poonindie Institution — Albany Institution—Warangesda—New Guinea . . . 67

CHAPTER VIII.

THE CHURCH IN NEW ZEALAND.

First intercourse between English and Maoris—Maori religion—Tapu—First Mission to New Zealand and its results—Bishop Selwyn—Maori uprisings—Maori Evangelists and Martyrs—Rev. J. C. Patteson—New Zealand Episcopate—The Kingmaker and the land question—Bishop Selwyn as mediator—War of races—Hau Hau fanaticism—Rev. C. S. Volkner—Fidelity of Maori Clergy—Declension of the race . . 83

CHAPTER IX.

MISSIONS IN THE PACIFIC OCEAN.

Melanesian Mission—Its origin and difficulties—Bishop Selwyn's first visit—Isle of Pines—Babel of tongues—Mission formally commenced—First pupils brought to New Zealand—Synod at Sydney—Mr. Patteson and the 'Southern Cross'—Nonconformist Missions; their success — Consecration of Rev. J. C. Patteson—Labour vessels—Bishop Patteson's death—Effect on the Mission and on public feeling—Rev.

J. R. Selwyn and Rev. J. Still—Mr. Selwyn consecrated Bishop—Native confidence recovered—Present state of the Mission—Fiji—Earlier Missions in Fiji—Hon. Sir A. H. Gordon — Hawaiian Islands — Idolatry abandoned — King Kamehameha IV.—English Mission founded—Disappointments—Progress—Bishop Wilberforce's forecast . . . 96

CHAPTER X.

THE CHURCH IN SOUTH AFRICA.

Dutch occupation—The English succeed—Inadequate spiritual provision—The Cape visited by Indian Bishops, and by the first Bishop of Tasmania—The first Bishop of Capetown—Kafirs—Diocese divided—Litigation—Grahamstown—Kafir delusion—Progress—Kaffraria—Bishop Merriman—Bishop Key—Natal—Bishop Colenso—Bishop Macrorie—Zululand—Orange Free State—Pretoria—St. Helena—Tristan d'Acunha—Mauritius: its variety of peoples—Madagascar—Early Missions—Persecution of Christians—The Island re-opened—An English Bishop sent—Native Ministry—The French Blockade 117

CHAPTER XI.

MISSIONS ON THE EASTERN COAST OF AFRICA.

The Church Missionary Society—Drs. Krapf and Rebmann—The Slave Trade—Dr. Livingstone—Bishop Mackenzie—His first settlement—His death—The Continent abandoned—Zanzibar—The Mission in difficulties—Work recommenced on the mainland—Lake Tanganyika and the London Missionary Society—Lake Nyanza—Mr. H. M. Stanley and King Mtesa—The C.M.S. Mission to Lake Nyanza—Death of King Mtesa—Disaster to Bishop Hannington and his party—The prospects of Central Africa 141

CHAPTER XII.

MISSIONS ON THE WESTERN COAST OF AFRICA.

Sierra Leone—Its unhealthiness—The Episcopate—Yoruba and the Niger—Abbeokuta—Bishop Crowther—Mohammedan cruelty — Liberia and Maryland — The American Church Mission — The Pongas Mission — Chief Wilkinson — Christianity and civilisation 152

CHAPTER XIII.

MISSIONS IN THE EAST INDIES.

Successive rulers of India — English possession — Early contact with Christianity in India — The Malabar Church — Danish Missions — Serampore Mission — English Church Missions — Conditions of Missionary work in India — Varieties of race and language — Antipathy to English — Strength of Non-Christian religions in India — Brahmanism — Buddhism — Mohammedanism — Truths in common — Hindrances to growth in India — Episcopate limited — Changes needed — Travancore — Tinnevelly 160

CHAPTER XIV.

MISSIONS IN THE EAST INDIES (*continued*).

Bishop Middleton — Bishop's College founded — Bishops Heber, Turner, and James — Sees of Madras and Bombay — Bishop Cotton (1857–1866) — Bishop Milman (1867–1876) — The Kôls — The Karens — Dioceses of Lahore and Rangoon — The Mutiny of 1857 — Delhi Mission destroyed and restored — The Cambridge Brotherhood — Missions of C.M.S. in North India — Bombay — Rangoon — Upper Burma and Mandalay Mission — Ceylon — South India — Devil worship — Self-help — Bishops in Tinnevelly — The famine and its teaching — Proportion of Christians to Non-Christians in India — Need of all kinds of Ministrations — Medical Missions — Education — Bazaar preaching — Domestic life and asceticism . . . 176

CHAPTER XV.

MISSIONS IN CHINA, JAPAN, AND BORNEO.

Difficulties in China — People — Languages — Religions — Roman Missions — The American Church Mission — The C.M.S. — The

Episcopate—The S.P.G.—China Inland Mission—Chinese converts in other lands—Japan—St. Francis Xavier—Japan opened by treaty—Latency of Christianity—Japanese converts—Bishops Poole and Bickersteth—Changed attitude of people towards Christianity—The Corea—Borneo—Bishop McDougall—Chinese in Borneo—North Borneo Company—Singapore—Sir S. Raffles 192

CHAPTER XVI.

CONCLUSION.

Retrospect—Financial administration—Contributions to Missions—Endowments—Universities and Colleges—Supply of Clergy—Organisation and administration—Failure of Letters Patent—Synodal action essential—Adopted in New Zealand, Australia, Canada, Africa, and West Indies—The Laity in Synods—Power of Synods—Lambeth Conferences—Autonomy of Colonial Churches—Summary—Encouragement or the reverse—Spread of English-speaking races, and its results—Spread of English Christianity and its results . 201

INDEX 217

THE ENGLISH CHURCH IN OTHER LANDS

OR THE

SPIRITUAL EXPANSION OF ENGLAND.

CHAPTER I.

GROWTH OF THE MISSIONARY SPIRIT.

THE story of England's contribution to the evangelisation of the world must to a great extent run in parallel lines with the story of her colonial development; but it will not be confined within those limits, wide and ever-extending as they are. The steady increase of our colonies has indeed supplied the most pressing call, and based our duty on the very obvious obligation of caring first for our own kindred; but the Christian conscience has taken a wider view, and has recognised the duty of spreading the knowledge of eternal Truth wherever the commerce of England has been spread. If the tale of the spiritual expansion of England is to be told, some review must first be taken of her territorial expansion. The two are very intimately united, and it will be found that, as in the growth of our colonial empire many elements have combined to make it what it is—diplomacy, war, adventure, greed, each having contributed its share—so in the building up of the Church in other lands there have been mixed motives, and by-ends, persecutions, ambitions, fanaticism, strangely mingled with the purer and nobler views of the Evangelist and the Christian statesman.

It is difficult to fix the exact date of the beginnings of our colonial empire. There were attempts and foreshadowings of it in the enterprises of Columbus and Cabot in the reign of Henry VII. These men discovered new lands; but no new settlements appear to have been made either on the Western Continent or in any of the adjacent islands under the commissions which the king had given. There was probably a fear of incurring the censure of the Church; for Pope Eugenius IV. had conferred on Portugal, about the middle of the fifteenth century, all lands that might at any time be discovered between Cape Non, seven degrees S. of Gibraltar, and the continent of India; and in 1493 the lands of the Western hemisphere were given by Pope Alexander VI. to the united kingdoms of Castile and Arragon.

Birth of the Colonial Empire

Henry VIII. made few attempts to discover or to acquire foreign possessions. His hands were full of other matters. France and Spain were powerful rivals abroad; and at home the conflicting interests, the violent agitations, and even formidable dangers which beset the Reformation movement fully occupied both king and subjects. Independent trading ventures were made, not without the cognisance of the king, to the coast of Guinea and to the Levant; but on Henry's death in 1547 Calais was the

Henry VIII. 1509-1547

sole foreign possession of England. The reign of Edward VI. saw many attempts made by merchants, under the direct sanction of the Crown, to force a passage by the north-east to Cathay, with the result of establishing factories at Moscow and Archangel and of incorporating in 1554 the Russia Company; but no land was acquired in foreign countries.

<small>Edward VI. 1547-1553</small>

In the reign of Elizabeth, Hawkins, Drake, and Cavendish visited the West Indies, South America, and Mexico; and Magellan won the honour of discovering the straits which still bear his name. Frobisher pushed his way into Hudson's Bay and returned with no abiding results. But in 1578 the first national attempt at distinct colonisation was made when Elizabeth gave to Humphrey Gilbert, a Devonshire knight, authority 'to take possession of all remote and barbarous lands unoccupied by any Christian prince or people.' The undertaking did not immediately succeed, but it paved the way for success. Newfoundland was occupied in 1584, but subsequently abandoned, and in the same year Virginia was founded but not retained. The original settlers were never again heard of, although the traditions of the natives, which are confirmed by the physical characteristics of the tribe of Hatteras Indians, point to their having been adopted by the sons of the forest.

<small>Colonisation in the reign of Elizabeth, 1558-1603</small>

The European nations were now competing with one another for the dominion of the known world. Portugal had established itself in India, in the Persian Gulf, on the peninsula of Malacca, on either shore of Africa, and in Brazil. It had possessed itself of the chief harbours of

<small>European nations and their colonial possessions</small>

Ceylon, and had formed settlements in Borneo, Java, and Sumatra. Its connection with China and Japan was commenced in this century, and its trade extended far beyond its territorial possessions. Spain had conquered Mexico, Peru, and Chili in the first half of the century, and before its close had seized on many of the possessions of her neighbour and rival. The Dutch Republic, at the close of the century, was in the first rank of commercial nations; and France had begun to lay the foundations of that extended dominion, which later on affected so powerfully the destinies of Europe. Thus it seemed as though England was to be outstripped by her rivals; for although in the last year of the century the East India Company received its charter, no permanent foreign settlements had yet been made, and her colonies were but the shadow of great things to come.

With the reign of James I. peace abroad and religious strife at home invited to colonisation the adventurous spirits of the time, as well as those who longed for a home remote from political and religious turbulence. The king gave a patent by which, in 1606, Virginia and New England were permanently settled. In 1620 a Puritan colony occupied Massachusetts. Five years later, the Royalists, seeing the cause of their sovereign daily becoming weaker, looked to other lands; and, in the words of an old chronicler, 'the calamities of England served to people Barbados,' to which island Cromwell afterwards banished his captives, Irish and English. In 1622, a colony was established in the French possession of Nova Scotia, which was not finally surrendered to England until 1713. In 1633 Charles I. gave Mary-

Colonisation in the reign of James I. 1603-1625

land to Lord Baltimore, who made it a Roman Catholic settlement; about the same time the Carolinas were bestowed on Lord Berkeley; Cromwell in 1655 wrested Jamaica from Spain; in 1664 New Amsterdam was taken from the Dutch and re-named New York; in 1670 the region surrounding Hudson's Bay was annexed and called Rupert's Land after Prince Rupert, the founder of the Hudson's Bay Company, which received its charter from the Crown in the following year. St. Helena, seized by the East India Company from the Dutch, was secured to the Company by Charles II., who condoned their offence in view of the great advantage of a resting-place on the long route to India being at the service of the country. Pennsylvania, purchased by William Penn of the Duke of York in 1682, became a place of refuge for the persecuted Quakers. Meanwhile the East India Company had been stealthily extending their possessions. In 1611 their factories were established at Madras; thirty years later they founded a settlement at Hooghly, which in 1698 was removed to Calcutta, then an insignificant village; in 1662 the Portuguese gave the town and island of Bombay as part of the dowry of Katharine, wife of Charles II., by whom it was made over to the East India Company. So the seventeenth century closed and left England in possession of large territories in India, in North America, and in the West Indies.

Charles I. 1625-1649
Cromwell, 1649-1662
Charles II. 1662-1685
East India Company
Colonisation in the eighteenth century.

Very early in the eighteenth century Gibraltar was taken; in 1713 the Treaty of Utrecht ceded to England Nova Scotia and Newfoundland; Canada was conquered in 1760, Prince

Edward's Island having been seized two years before. Sierra Leone was acquired in 1787, the native chiefs gladly ceding their rights in return for the protection of England; in 1787 New South Wales promised in some degree to atone for the loss of the American colonies which had declared their independence; in 1795 the British took all the Dutch possessions in Ceylon and shortly afterwards seized the whole island, making it a separate colony; the conquest of Trinidad in 1797 closes the list of territories acquired in the eighteenth century.

In 1806 the Cape of Good Hope was taken from the Dutch, and in 1810 Mauritius was won from the French. The Treaty of Paris in 1814 secured our possession of Guiana. Singapore was acquired in 1819, the Falkland Islands in 1833. In 1840 Natal was taken from the Dutch, and in the same year New Zealand became a colony under the terms of the Waitangi treaty with the Maoris. In 1846 the island of Labuan was ceded, and in 1874 the Fiji Islands were, as they remain, the latest addition to our colonial possessions; unless, indeed, Cyprus, which was assigned by the Sultan of Turkey to England in 1878 for 'occupation and administration,' may be placed in the same category as the colonies proper.

<small>and in the nineteenth century</small>

Thus has been gathered together that 'aggregation of territorial atoms' which an American statesman declared to be 'a power to which Rome in the height of her glory was not to be compared.' From many centres the colonies have spread and threaten already to set out on fresh ventures of acquisition for themselves, while the withdrawals of the charters of the East India Company and of the Hudson's

<small>The colonial empire</small>

Bay Company have opened up new regions, as territories of the former company, now under the direct rule of the Crown, extend from Cape Comorin to the Himalayas, while Rupert's Land has changed from a vast hunting-ground to the most fertile wheat-growing country in the world.

Turning to the spiritual side of the work of these early discoverers and colonisers, we may say of it as Lord Bacon said of the Spaniards' discoveries in the Western World: 'It cannot be affirmed, if one speak ingenuously, that it was the propagation of the Christian faith that was the adamant of that discovery, entry, and plantation, but gold and silver and temporal profit and glory; so that what was first in God's providence was but second in man's appetite and intention.'

<small>The spiritual growth of the colonies</small>

Nevertheless in the earlier expeditions the thirst for gold was not the sole motive. Frobisher's expedition was accompanied by a clergyman, 'Master Wolfall,' who had been preacher to Her Majesty's Council, and who being 'well seated and settled at home with a good and large living, having a good honest woman to wife and very towardly children,' went on the voyage of danger in the hope of 'saving souls and reforming infidels to Christianity.' On reaching the American shores 'he celebrated a communion on land, at the partaking whereof was the captain and many other gentlemen and soldiers, mariners and miners, with him. The celebration of the Divine mysteries was the first signe, seale, and confirmation of Christ's name, death, and passion, ever known in these quarters.'[1]

<small>Frobisher's expedition</small>

[1] Hakluyt.

Sir Humphrey Gilbert set forth as the most prominent motive for acquiring the full possession of these 'so ample and pleasant countries for the Crown and people of England' 'the honour of God and compassion of poor infidels led captive by the Devil.' In the charter given by James I. to the Virginia Company it was provided that 'the word and service of God be preached, planted, and used, not only in the said colony, but, as much as may be, among the savages bordering among them, according to the rites and doctrine of the Church of England.' The Rev. Robert Hunt was appointed to accompany the expedition. Raleigh, though his fortune was gone, yet gave 100*l*. to the Virginia Company for the establishment of religion in the colony; and the names of Lord Delawarr, of Whitaker, son of a master of St. John's College, Cambridge, of Sandys, the pupil of Hooker, and of the saintly Nicholas Ferrar, who were influential members of the company, are a guarantee that other than commercial motives prompted the venture. The baptism of Pocahontas, daughter of the native chief, and her subsequent marriage to an English gentleman who brought her to England, are familiar to all.

The Commonwealth was not less mindful of religion than had been the Monarchy. In 1648 'the Commons of England assembled in Parliament, having received intelligence that the heathens in New England are beginning to call upon the name of the Lord, feel bound to assist in the work.' This was the preamble of the charter given to the New England Company, the forerunner of all missionary societies, which still continues to expend the annual

<small>The Commonwealth's care for religion</small>

interest of its endowments on the support of ministers of religion, having received a second charter from Charles II. and been regulated by three Decrees of Chancery in 1792, 1808, and 1836 respectively.

Charles II. established, soon after his accession, a 'Council of Foreign Plantations,' which sat in the Star Chamber at Westminster; and among other things the Council was directed 'to take care to propagate the Gospel; to send strict orders and instructions for regulating and reforming the debaucheries of planters and servants; to consider how the natives, or such as have been purchased from other parts to be servants or slaves, may be best invited to the Christian faith.'

<small>Council of Foreign Plantation, temp. Charles II.</small>

At this time—1662—the Church of England began to pray daily, morning and evening, for all sorts and conditions of men, that God would be pleased to make His ways known unto them, His saving health among all nations. A hundred years had passed since the Reformation settlement, and the Prayer-book had not contained a word of prayer for the conversion of the heathen except the collect for Good Friday, which was offered on only one day in the year. The Church's conscience was now awakened by the activity of discoverers and adventurers. Her ministers were beginning to follow their flocks into other lands; but nearly fifty years had yet to lapse before the Church of England could point to a single foreign mission. Robert Boyle, who had offered in 1661 to lead a company of evangelists to New England, foiled in his desire, endowed in 1691 the lectureships which still bear his name, with the intention that they

<small>The Church and the prayer for 'all conditions of men'</small>

'should prove the Christian religion against Atheists, Theists, Pagans, Jews, and Mahometans, and be assisting to all companies and encouraging them in any undertakings for propagating the Christian religion in foreign parts.' He also left by will the residue of his estate to a society which was called and is still known as the 'Christian Faith Society for the advancement of the Christian religion amongst infidels in Virginia.' The Court of Chancery has more than once intervened in the operations of this society, whose funds are now applied to the benefit of the British West India Islands and the Mauritius. In this respect the colonisation of the seventeenth century compares favourably with that of the eighteenth— religion was never lost sight of; in many, indeed in the majority of cases, it held a prominent position ; in some it was the very cause of the whole undertaking. The colonisation of later times is in strange and painful contrast with the fervid zeal of the seventeenth century. Yet did this very zeal work infinite divisions and bitterness. The review of the religious condition of the various colonies gave deep concern to all thoughtful persons. In Barbados the authorities had divided the island into parishes, building in each a church, and taxing every acre with the payment of one pound of tobacco annually for the support of the clergyman. 'Opinionated and self-conceited persons who have declared an absolute dislike to the government of the Church of England were made to conform.' Masters of families were compelled to read prayers daily, morning and evening, and attendance at church on every Sunday was compulsory on those who lived within two miles of their

Boyle's Lectures

parish church, a fine of ten pounds of cotton being the penalty of neglect. New England, whose first settlers were Churchmen, who established themselves on the river Kenebec, became in 1620 the home of the Pilgrim Fathers. Massachusetts was a Puritan colony; but the settlers professed intense admiration and love for the Church which they described as 'our dear mother, ever acknowledging that such hope and part as we have received in the common salvation, we have obtained in her bosom.' Nevertheless they shortly afterwards established their own creed by law and tolerated no other. Strange, indeed, it is that the people who had made such noble sacrifices for liberty of conscience, soon came to regard the exercise of the civil power in enforcing uniformity to be only a righteous and godly procedure. For the natives they did nothing; indeed, they applied themselves to the task of the extirpation of 'the paynim, whom probably the Devil decoyed hither in hopes that the Gospel would never come here to disturb or to destroy his absolute reign over them.' The neglect of these poor people touched the heart of John Eliot, who patiently gave twelve years to the acquisition of their language, and then by his labours won for all time the honoured name of 'The Apostle of the Indians.'

Such a medley of faiths the world had never seen. In the southern colonies the Church was established by law; Romanists were the majority in Maryland; Pennsylvania was occupied by Quakers; Presbyterians and Baptists colonised New Jersey; Lutherans and Moravians from Germany abounded in

<small>Religious differences</small>

Carolina and Georgia; but these did not arrive until the next century.

At home there succeeded to long strife a period of frivolity and indifference, in which the few earnest spirits, who leavened the age in which they lived, looked on with dismay at the miscarriage of the designs which Raleigh and his contemporaries had formed for the extension of religion. Sir Leoline Jenkins now founded the Missionary Fellowships at Jesus College, Oxford, the holders of which were bound to service in foreign lands. A scheme for the support of a bishop in Virginia, who should be maintained out of the customs levied in the colony, was seriously entertained. Meanwhile the Bishop of London (Compton) sent Dr. Blair as his commissary to Virginia in 1683, and Dr. Bray in a similar capacity to Maryland in 1695. Their representations, especially those of Dr. Bray, were made public. Dr. Bray was impressed by the poverty and scanty knowledge of the clergy who had been sent, or were likely to go to America. He had made the following condition before going to Maryland as commissary: 'That since none but the poorer sort of clergy, who could not sufficiently supply themselves with books, could be persuaded to leave their friends, and change their country for one so remote, and that without a competent provision of books they could not answer the ends of their mission; if their lordships the Bishops thought fit to assist him in providing Parochial Libraries for the ministers that should be sent, he would be content to accept the commissary's office in Maryland.'

Missionary zeal in England.

Drs. Blair and Bray.

His proposal was cordially approved, and a document

signed by Archbishops Tenison and Sharpe and Bishops Compton, Lloyd, Patrick, and Moore, is still preserved in Lambeth Palace library, formally sanctioning the scheme for founding parochial libraries for the benefit of the clergy. In his journeys about England seeking to obtain subscriptions for his libraries as well as persons who might be willing to go to Maryland, he was frequently struck by the poverty of the clergy and the dearth of theological books; and he added to his scheme the establishment of such libraries in England and Wales. In Maryland he helped the Government in the division of the country into parishes. On returning to England, so ardent was his desire to see standard and useful works placed within the reach of the clergy and laity, that he may be considered to have been in 1698 the main founder of the Society for Promoting Christian Knowledge.

Not from America alone were claims pressing on the attention of the Church. In 1694 Dean Prideaux published a scheme for the conversion of India. If it produced no other immediate result than the recognition by the Legislature, in the renewal of the Company's charter four years later, of the duty incumbent on them of providing 'in every garrison or superior factory one minister and one decent and convenient place for divine service only,' it was not a failure. But it did more: the Government expressly enacted 'that such ministers as should be sent to reside in India should apply themselves to learn the language of the country, the better to enable them to instruct the Gentoos, who should be the servants of the Company or their agents, in the Protestant religion.'

Dean Prideaux and the E. I. Company

The Society for Promoting Christian Knowledge had not been long in existence when the necessity of an organisation more formally constituted, which should undertake, as the Church's instrument and representative, the actual initiation and direction of missionary work, was perceived. The Christian Knowledge Society employed no missionaries or ordained agents, but limited its functions to the duties specified in its title. Accordingly on March 13, 1701, the Lower House of the Convocation of Canterbury, assembled in Henry VII.'s Chapel at Westminster, appointed a committee 'ad inquirendum in ea, quæ sibi videbuntur maxime idonea, pro Christianâ Religione in Plantationibus (ut vocant) sive coloniis transmarinis ad hoc regnum Angliæ quovis modo spectantibus, promovendâ.' The Archbishop of Canterbury (Tenison), acting on this, applied to the Crown for a Royal Charter; and on June 16, 1701, the Society for the Propagation of the Gospel was thus incorporated. It immediately commenced its work at Archangel and Moscow, and extended its operations to America in 1702, to Newfoundland in 1703, to the West Indies in 1732, to Nova Scotia in 1749, and to Western Africa in 1752. From the first, it aimed at the conversion of the pagans as well as the benefit of Christian emigrants and colonists; but its income was very limited, never exceeding 6,000*l.* in any year of the first century of its existence. It was a century of much apathy, and at home and abroad men's thoughts were occupied with other things than the spread of the Gospel.

In the second half of the century the loyalty of the

colonists showed signs of wavering. In India as well as in America, wars were carried on to the glory of our arms and the increase of our possessions, but at infinite cost and strain of our strength and resources. In the reign of Queen Anne it had been purposed to send out four bishops, two to the West Indies and two to America, but the project ended with the Queen's death. The Church seemed powerless and unable to help herself. America demanded bishops, and demanded them in vain. The solitary missionary instrument of the Church was poor and without patronage. The famous Bishop Butler declined the offer of the Archbishopric of Canterbury, alleging that it was too late to save a falling Church. Nonconformity was weak and persecuted, and the prevalent Calvinism of the day did not incite to missionary work. The Danish mission had sent noble representatives to Tranquebar in 1714. In 1732 the patient Moravians from their home in Silesia began to send out members of their body to the West Indies, North and South America, Lapland, Tartary, Western and Southern Africa. In 1769, the Wesleyan Society began in America the work which has been since extended to all parts of the world. In 1792, Carey, the son of a shoemaker in Northamptonshire, destined to prove one of the greatest of Indian missionaries, moved the Baptist sect, of which he was a member, to establish missions. He was met with many objections: proposing for discussion at a meeting of ministers 'the duty of attempting to spread the Gospel among the heathen,' he was at once rebuked and told that if God wished to convert the heathen He could do it without human aid. But he persevered and got together a society which works in the East and West Indies, West Africa, and China. In 1794, the Congregationalists established the London Missionary Society, the scene of whose work lies in India, South Africa, the West Indies, the Pacific, and Madagascar. On April 12, 1799, sixteen clergymen met at the Castle and Falcon Tavern in Aldersgate Street, and, moved by the consideration that not a single clergyman had yet gone to either of the great continents of Africa and Asia, they founded what was called 'The Society for The C. M. S. Missions to Africa and the East,' a title which was afterwards changed to 'The Church Missionary Society for Africa and the East.' The work of this society is by no means limited to the regions set forth in its title; since its establishment in 1800 it has enlarged its sphere as its means have increased, and its name is familiar in every part of the globe whither its representatives have gone.

Thus the eighteenth century closed with greatly multiplied missionary machinery, and with widely extended fields of work; but the first twenty years of the following century were not a period marked by much zeal or corresponding progress. The Church at home was struggling to make up for past neglect, and to build churches in which to gather alienated and indifferent multitudes. Of machinery there was enough, possibly too much; what was wanted was direction and guidance. For the Colonial Church these were supplied by Bishop Blomfield. He saw the colonies increasing and spreading in all directions; yet there were only ten colonial bishops in 1841—four in North America, three in the East Indies, two in the West Indies, and one in Australia, and these were in the majority of cases stipendiaries of the Government. The statesman-bishop exposed the presbyterianism of the Church, thus left without episcopal rule; and on Whitsun Tuesday, 1841, the assembled bishops of England, Ireland, and Scotland, at his intervention, sent out a famous declaration which launched the Colonial Bishoprics Council. The ten bishoprics of 1841 have now, in 1886, reached the number of 75, and it may be convenient to the reader to have the following table of their names, their locality, and the date of their foundation:—

In NORTH AMERICA: Nova Scotia, 1787; Quebec, 1793; Toronto, 1839; Newfoundland, 1839; Fredericton, 1845; Montreal, 1850; Huron, 1857; Ontario, 1862; Algoma, 1873; Niagara, 1875; Rupert's Land, 1849; Moosonee, 1872; Saskatchewan, 1874; Mackenzie River, 1874; Qu'Appelle, 1884; Athabasca, 1884; Columbia, 1859; Caledonia, 1879; New Westminster, 1879.

In ASIA: Calcutta, 1814; Madras, 1835; Bombay, 1837; Lahore, 1877; Rangoon, 1877; Travancore, and Cochin, 1879; Colombo, 1845; Singapore, 1855; Victoria, 1849; Mid China, 1872; North China, 1880; Japan, 1883; Jerusalem, 1841.

In AUSTRALIA: Sydney, 1836; Tasmania, 1842; Adelaide, 1847; Melbourne, 1847; Newcastle, 1847; Perth, 1857; Brisbane, 1859; Goulburn, 1863; Grafton and Armidale, 1867; Bathurst, 1869; Ballaarat, 1875; North Queensland, 1878; Riverina, 1883.

In NEW ZEALAND and the PACIFIC: Auckland,

1841; Christchurch, 1856; Nelson, 1858; Wellington, 1858; Waiapu, 1858; Melanesia, 1861; Dunedin, 1871; Honolulu, 1861.

In the WEST INDIES and SOUTH AMERICA: Jamaica, 1824; Barbados, 1824; Antigua, 1842; Guiana, 1842; Nassau, 1861; Trinidad, 1872; Falkland Islands, 1869.

In AFRICA: Capetown, 1847; Grahamstown, 1853; Maritzburg, 1853; St. John's, 1873; Bloemfontein, 1863; Zululand, 1870; Pretoria, 1878; St. Helena, 1859; Mauritius, 1854; Madagascar, 1874; Central Africa, 1861; Eastern Equatorial Africa, 1884; Sierra Leone, 1852; Niger, 1864.

To this list must be added the See of Gibraltar, which was founded in 1842.

It should also be stated that the Church of the United States, which sprang from the Church of England, since the political severance of the two countries in 1784, when it obtained the episcopate by the consecration of Bishop Seabury at Aberdeen, has raised the number of her bishops to sixty-seven, whose dioceses cover the continent from the Atlantic to the Pacific, and has also planted missions, with bishops at their head, in China, in Japan, and on the West Coast of Africa.

Growth of the Church of the United States

Since 1841, three new missionary organisations have been formed, viz. the Patagonian, now called the South American Missionary Society, the Colonial and Continental Church Society, and the Universities Mission to Central Africa. Several small associations or guilds have also been formed for the purpose either of carrying on independent work or of assisting work previously existing. But enough space

Modern missionary societies

has been given to machinery; it will be the object of the following chapters to show what the machinery has produced, either of actual result or of future promise.

CHAPTER II.

THE CHURCH IN THE UNITED STATES OF AMERICA.

At the commencement of the eighteenth century there were not a score of clergymen of the English Church ministering outside the limits of this country; nor was Nonconformity more fully represented. The colonies on the American continent were growing rapidly in wealth and numbers. Their whole population was about 1,200,000 whites and 250,000 negroes, while the population of the mother country did not much exceed 6,000,000. The population of Virginia had doubled itself in twenty-five years; but for the first seventy-five years of its existence not a single place of worship was erected in this the foremost colony, largely populated by Churchmen. Of worldly prosperity there was every token; Virginia was a vast tobacco plantation; Georgia and the Carolinas boasted of their crops of maize, rice, and indigo; while New York, Pennsylvania, and the New England Colonies obtained their wealth from their fisheries, their woods, and their cornfields. The colonists had brought with them each their own religious creed with its peculiar shibboleths, and these again were divided and subdivided into a variety of sects.

Early settlement

On April 24, 1702, the Society for the Propagation

of the Gospel sent forth its first representatives, the Rev. George Keith and Patrick Gordon, who landed at Boston on June 11. They were shortly followed by many more. So novel a display of zeal on the part of the Church attracted attention. Among others the Rev. J. Wesley, Rector of Epworth, in Lincolnshire, and father of the founder of Methodism, was much interested, and put himself in communication with the authorities. The religious society which he had founded in his parish shared his feelings, and was especially moved by the news which came from Tranquebar of the Danish Mission established there. Mr. Wesley died in 1735, but his sons were not a whit behind their father in missionary zeal. John was urged by Dr. Burton, President of Corpus Christi College, who had observed his career at Oxford, to go to Georgia and to take his brother Charles with him. They sailed on October 13, 1735; and for two years John Wesley was on the list of the missionaries of the Propagation Society in Georgia, Charles having gone on to Frederica. Their ministry was not successful; in the words of Southey, John Wesley, 'instead of regarding his people as babes in the progress of their Christian life to be fed with milk instead of strong meat, drenched them with the physic of an intolerant discipline.' In 1737, he shook off the dust of his feet and left Georgia in bitter disappointment. His connection with America did not cease; the work which he carried on for fifty years in England was renewed in Pennsylvania and other States. The War of Independence arrested it for a time; his 'calm address to the Americans,' written before the war actually broke out, excited much resentment against him, but on the restoration of peace his

John and Charles Wesley

preachers renewed their activity, and on September 2, 1784, only a few weeks before the consecration of the first American bishop, he 'set apart,' at Bristol, 'by the imposition of hands, Thomas Coke to be superintendent of the flock of Christ,' justifying his action on the ground that he despaired of the Church sending bishops to America.

The slaves and the Indians had occupied a large place in the sympathies of thoughtful men both at home and in the colonies. The first mention of slavery occurs in the annals of Virginia, where in 1620 twenty negroes are recorded to have been purchased by the settlers in Jamestown from a Dutch ship which had put in there for the purposes of trade. Bishop Gibson, who held the See of London from 1723 to 1748, wrote and published exhortations to masters of families to 'encourage and promote the instruction of their negroes in the Christian faith,' and to the clergy to observe the same duty in their several parishes. Bishop Wilson published in 1740 his famous 'Essay toward an Instruction for the Indians' in the form of twenty dialogues between an Indian and a missionary. Bishop Berkeley for years struggled to carry out his magnificent scheme for a college in the Bermudas for the education of a clergy and 'for the better supplying of churches in our Foreign Plantations and for converting the savages to Christianity.' He looked forward to the establishment of bishoprics in each Colonial Church; and this question, which now became urgent, was insisted upon with increasing pertinacity until the Declaration of Independence.

The slaves

Churchmanship and loyalty to the Crown had

hitherto been synonymous: two clergymen had received consecration from one of the Nonjuror bishops, but they had been withdrawn from the colonies in the interests of peace. The Declaration of Independence, made in July 1776, had been preceded by a time of great persecution of the Church and especially of the clergy. Many fled over the border into Nova Scotia, while others remained at the place of danger and duty. Charles Inglis, rector of Trinity Church, New York, was conspicuous as a confessor: although his church was ordered to be closed, he continued to visit the sick, to comfort the distressed, to baptize, and to bury the dead. He refused to give up the keys of his church, and persisted in praying for the sovereign, although more than a hundred armed men occupied the building and threatened to shoot him if the obnoxious prayer were offered. His church was burned to the ground, his person banished, and his estate confiscated. When in 1783 peace was restored, the Church in Virginia had become wasted and almost destroyed. Of 164 churches, which existed before the war, many were in ruins, and the number of the clergy was reduced from 91 to 28.

Persecution of Churchmen

The importunate and even passionate demands for an episcopate, which had for so many years been made, had been contemptuously rejected; but the same stroke which severed thirteen colonies from England, set the Church free to obtain for herself bishops of her own. The Church in Connecticut, as soon as peace was secured, sent Dr. Samuel Seabury to England to obtain consecration. Political difficulties were suggested; and on November 14, 1784,

Consecration of Bishop Seabury, 1784

he was consecrated at Aberdeen by three Scottish Bishops. Three years later Bishop White of Pennsylvania and Bishop Provoost of New York were consecrated in Lambeth Palace; and in 1788 a bishop was consecrated for Virginia.

The progress of the Church of the United States has been very remarkable. Its first Convention was held in Holy Trinity Church, Philadelphia, in 1784,

<small>First Convention of the Church in America</small> and after the lapse of an eventful century the same building witnessed the Convention of 1883. Its Liturgy differs in some material points from the Prayer Book of the Church of England. Its Eucharistic Office is more closely on the lines of the Scottish Office; while in some respects the Prayer Book is so inferior to our own that the Convention has recently taken steps to provide for its 'enrichment.' It is no small glory to any Church to have kept pace with the rapid development of the United States, and this credit may certainly be given to it. It has sent out its bishops to new States almost in advance of the wave of immigration, and it has stood between the settlers and the Indian population and has nobly cared for the red men.

The Indians had all along been cared for by the English clergy of the Propagation Society, and in the <small>Conversion of the Indian races</small> War of Independence their loyalty was conspicuous. The 'Six-Nation Confederacy' fought gallantly on the side of the British, and Mohawks and Oneidas are everywhere mentioned in the records of the period as brave and Christian races. The American Church has not only taught and cared for the Indians; it has followed them in their wanderings. In other regions the natives have been invited to occupy reserves; and on their settling down, and giving up their nomadic habits, the Church has professed its readiness to teach them. But in the far western States the clergy have shared their wandering lives; and when they have accepted the total change of manners, which only the Gospel can produce, they have proved themselves capable of becoming industrious and peaceful settlers. Few nobler stories can be told than the tale of the missionary's work under such bishops as Bishop Whipple of Minnesota, and the Bishops of Nebraska and Dakota. Again, at Utah, in the very stronghold of the Mormonite imposture, a famous bishop (Tuttle) pitched his tent, though his life was threatened by the 500,000 victims of this superstition; but he found many, who had been lured from the rural parishes of England to the Salt Lake City, thankful to escape and to return to the Church of their fathers.

The absolute freedom of this Church to enlarge its borders and to increase its episcopate has been nobly used. It would have been a splendid effort to have kept pace with the rapid settlement of new lands, and with the extraordinary influx of population over the vast area of the American Union; this the Church has done, but it has done more. A continent might well have seemed a sufficiently ample field for the zeal and the energy of a young Church, with few wealthy members; but so long ago as 1844 (five years before the mother Church followed her example), the American Church sent a bishop to China, although the treaty which opened the ports of that empire was not completed. In 1851 it sent a bishop to Cape Palmas, on the West Coast of Africa, and in 1874 it gave to

Growth of the American Church

Japan its first Anglican bishop. Of the work of these prelates and their brethren mention will be made in the proper place.

The relations between the mother country and the United States were never so cordial as they are now. That such sentiments between the two great branches of the English-speaking race should continue and increase must be the earnest prayer of every man who desires the best and truest interests of humanity. It may be open to doubt whether the bonds which unite nations the most firmly are those which are forged by commerce and diplomacy; haply a common faith is the most potent and abiding link. Certainly the feeling of American Churchmen towards the mother land and the mother Church is one of reverent and passionate affection. To the great gatherings assembled under the Archbishop of Canterbury at Lambeth in 1867 and in 1878, the American bishops came in large numbers, and their influence was recognised and welcomed. More recently, six bishops and many of their clergy came, as on a sacred pilgrimage, to keep at Aberdeen the centenary of Seabury's consecration; and on the actual anniversary, November 14, 1884, they were present at a service in St. Paul's Cathedral, where the Gospel was read by a grandson of Seabury, and the sermon was preached by the Archbishop of Canterbury. Nor have signs of brotherly sympathy been wanting on the side of England. Two English bishops at least have attended the Triennial Conventions of the American Church, where the Canadian Church has frequently been represented by its bishops; and in 1871, on the occasion of the late Bishop Selwyn's

Intercourse between the Churches of England and America

visit, it was determined to make an offering of a magnificent alms-dish, which, kept among the muniments and treasures of Lambeth, should be for all time a token of the affection of the daughter to the mother Church. This was presented on July 3, 1872, Bishop McIlvaine of Ohio and Bishop Selwyn each holding it in one hand, and on bended knees offering it to the Archbishop of Canterbury.

There was a beautiful sentiment in the practice of the Greeks more than two thousand years ago, when the leaders of each colonisation venture, as they went forth to found new homes in distant lands, took with them from the common home and altar of the mother State some of the sacred fire, which henceforth would never be allowed to die out, but would burn on in token of unity with the ancestral flame from which it had been borne away. It was the teaching of heathenism, which Christianity is bound to interpret—that only in the clanship of the temple and of the altar can be found the links which will bind together nations whom thousands of leagues separate.

CHAPTER III.

THE CHURCH IN NEWFOUNDLAND, NOVA SCOTIA, QUEBEC, AND ONTARIO.

To the French belongs the honour of having first colonised Nova Scotia, now one of the oldest and most firmly established of the colonies of England. In 1598 the first body of French immigrants landed; and from that time until 1714, when by the

Early settlements

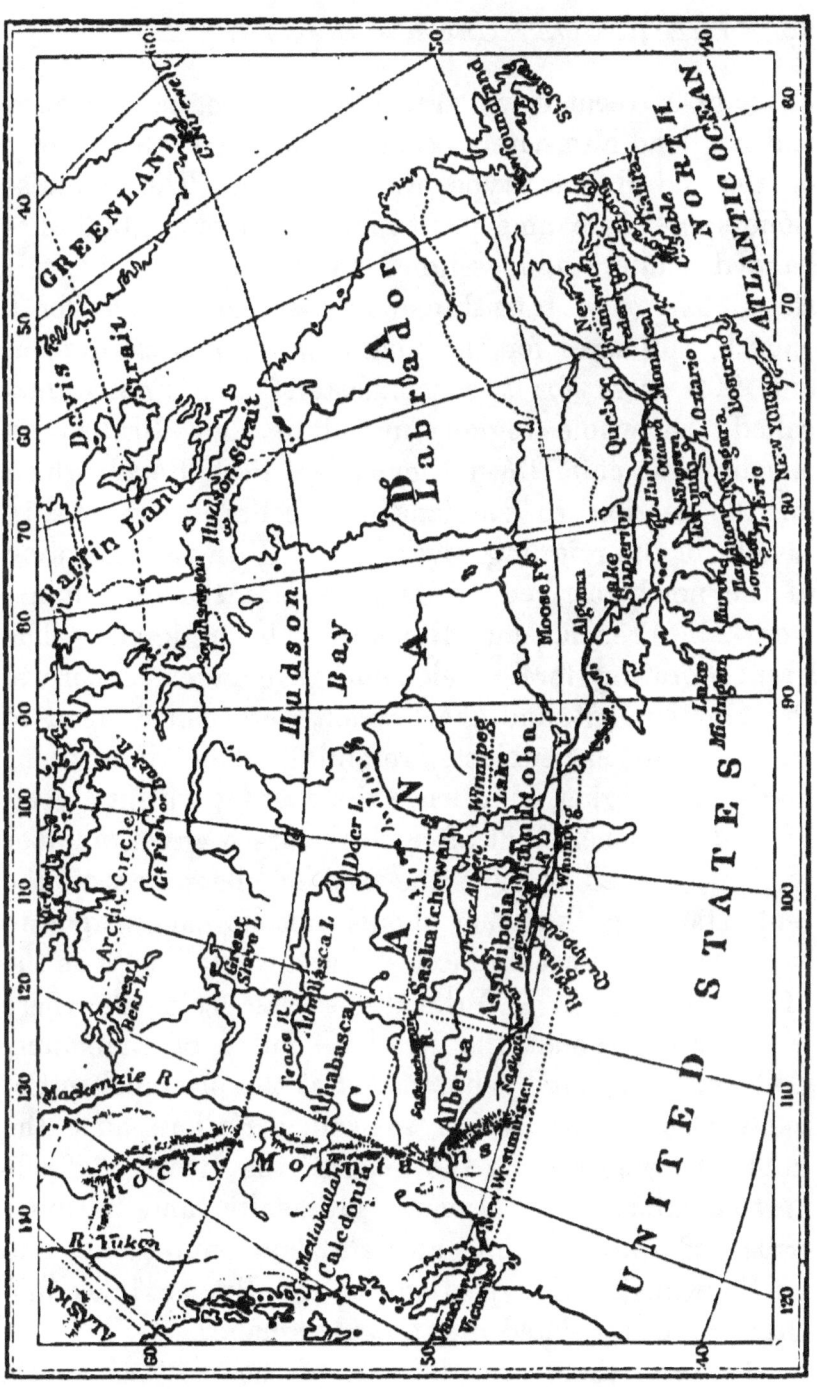

Peace of Utrecht it was transferred to England, France and England alternately occupied it. In 1749 a colony of the old Roman type was founded. The commissioners of trade and plantations sent out 4,000 disbanded soldiers and assigned to them land and townships. To each township was assigned a site for a church, 400 acres for the maintenance of a clergyman, and 200 acres for a schoolmaster. The French had called the whole region, including New Brunswick, Acadia; the chief town they called Port Royal, which on the cession to England was called Annapolis, in honour of the reigning sovereign. With the exception of the newly arrived military settlers, the inhabitants were all French, and Romanists by religion. The preponderating foreign element gave much concern to the Government, and the French were called upon to become British subjects, retaining their possessions and their religion, or to leave the country within a year. They did neither; but after five years a great number were persuaded to take the oath of allegiance, on the understanding that they should not be called upon to carry arms against France. These were known as the 'Neutral French.' With the soldier colonists there landed a clergyman, the Rev. W. Tutty, of Emmanuel College, Cambridge, who resided at the principal settlement, 'Cheductoo,' which was called Halifax, after the nobleman who was at the head of the Board of Trade at that time. The Micmac, Marashite, and Caribboo tribes of Indians were powerful and numerous, and for their instruction portions of the Prayer Book and Bible were translated into their languages.

In 1755 there occurred one of the most cruel acts

which have ever disgraced a civilised government. The
The Acadians Acadians to the number of about 18,000 were leading frugal and pious lives, cultivating their farms and dwelling in peace with all men; but they were suspected of favouring French designs on the country and were disarmed. Subsequently, when the fortunes of war went against the British, the presence of Neutrals was considered to be dangerous, and it was determined to remove them. Plans were laid in profound secrecy; the peasants unsuspectingly laboured at the gathering in of the harvest which they would never enjoy. On September 9 all the men and boys of ten years of age were ordered to assemble at their parish churches 'to be informed of His Majesty's intentions with respect to them.' The terrible decree was read that 'their lands and tenements, cattle of all kinds, and stock of every description were forfeited to the Crown, and they with only their money and their household goods were to be removed from the province.' Some escaped to the woods and found among the Indians the shelter which the English denied to them; some were hunted by the soldiers; some had to surrender through stress of hunger; but 7,000 Acadians were carried away to the different British colonies. Some returned after the restoration of peace and resumed their pastoral habits. In 1762 France resigned her claims, and the colony has since thriven without interruption. The melancholy story furnished the poet Longfellow with the subject-matter of his 'Evangeline.'

The War of Independence gave to Nova Scotia a large accession of population, which raised it to a high degree of importance. By the close of the year 1783,

30,000 refugees from Boston, New York, and other States had found sanctuary in a British colony. They were loyalists and had suffered much for their allegiance; they were also in the main members of the English Church. Their clergy accompanied them; and, encouraged by the fact that so long ago as 1758 the English Liturgy had been declared by local enactment to be 'the fixed form of worship' in Nova Scotia, eighteen clergymen on March 5, 1783, addressed to Sir Guy Carleton, then Governor of New York, a petition that a bishopric should be established in their colony. The governor supported their petition, not only as reasonable but on grounds of policy, as 'greatly conducive to the permanent loyalty and future tranquillity of a colony which is chiefly to consist of loyal exiles driven from their native provinces on account of their attachment to the British Constitution.' The petition was favourably received; and, in August 1787, Letters Patent were issued which conferred on the first colonial bishop a flood of spiritual and ecclesiastical authority, and gave to him coercive jurisdiction with power to suspend and deprive the clergy. The motive evidently was to reproduce in the colony the English hierarchy and to weld together by the exercise of the Royal prerogative an Imperial Church Establishment, bound by ties of interest and loyalty to support the throne, from which its authority was derived. The law officers were desired to report whether the sovereign could give the new bishop an *ex officio* place in the Legislative Council, analogous with the seats of English bishops in the House of Lords. They reported that this would not be lawful, but that each bishop might on his appointment be

[margin: Loyalist refugees in Nova Scotia]

summoned to the council personally and by name; and this for some time was done.

The first bishop, consecrated on August 12, 1787, was Dr. Charles Inglis, already mentioned as having borne noble witness to the truth when rector of Holy Trinity Church, New York. He was the first colonial bishop, and Nova Scotia is the first on the roll of the seventy-five sees in the colonies and missions of the English Church. His jurisdiction included all the British possessions in America, from Newfoundland to Lake Superior, an area about three times as large as Great Britain, and the total number of his clergy was twenty-four. Bishop Inglis laboured for twenty-nine years, making visitations which, in the then condition of the country, were often perilous, and watching over King's College, Windsor, which had been founded by George III. in 1770. In 1793 he was relieved of the charge of Upper and Lower Canada by the foundation of the see of Quebec, to which Dr. Jacob Mountain was consecrated; but, notwithstanding this relief, the bishop was not able to visit Newfoundland, which never saw a bishop until 1816. A further subdivision of the diocese was made in 1839, when that island became a separate diocese, and again in 1845, when the Right Rev. John Medley was consecrated Bishop of Fredericton.

The first Colonial Bishop, 1787

Newfoundland—which has never been amalgamated with Canada either for civil or for ecclesiastical purposes, but remains outside the Dominion under its own governor, and outside the Provincial Synod, its bishop holding mission direct from the See of Canterbury—is an island about the size of Ireland.

Newfoundland

It has been described as 'a rough shore with no interior.' There is not a human habitation beyond the immediate neighbourhood of the coast, which, with its endless succession of coves, inlets, and bays, enveloped very often in mist and fog, gives a home and harvest-field of water to a race of pious and hardy fishermen. In no part of the world are the conditions of life harder. A long winter and a sterile soil forbid aught but the simplest efforts at husbandry; the stormy seas offer in the summer months a livelihood obtained at the cost of much risk. Amid the icebergs and floes of the Arctic Sea the crews find the seals, which are to them the most fruitful source of income. In religion the mass of the people are nearly equally divided between Romanists and English Churchmen, the Wesleyans being the religious body of next importance.

Such a diocese not only demands a bishop of its own, but must be dealt with according to its particular needs. *The work of the Bishops* For more than half the year visitations cannot be made; and a bishop who wishes to make his office a reality must compress his travelling into about four months in each year, when the waters are open. Bishop Spencer, who first occupied the see from 1839 to 1843, hardly did more than gain experience and prepare his plans. He was succeeded by the apostolic Bishop Feild, whose simple life and unwearied toil, continued to his death in 1876, are a glory of the whole Church. In a small schooner, called 'the Hawk,' with the Church flag flying at her peak, this good bishop year after year made his way into remote creeks and bays, visiting people who had for the greater part of their lives been far beyond the reach of Church and priest, baptizing adults and children, and giving the blessing of the Church to those who had been living in wedlock, but not in the bonds of marriage. He found twelve clergymen settled in the larger harbours; but as time went on, the whole of the coastline was dotted with churches. Even on the barren shores of Labrador, where only the patient Moravians had ever carried the Word of God, he was able to place clergymen, who, moved by his example and filled with his spirit, gave themselves up to the banishment of that region. When, in 1876, he was called to his rest, he left in the diocese, which he had served so well, between seventy and eighty churches, and fifty clergymen, with the choir and transepts of a dignified cathedral, which the people have since completed as the most suitable memorial of his faithful episcopate. His example and his teaching will long remain. He attracted to his side many remarkable men. Some offered high intellectual and spiritual gifts, as well as worldly goods; others, less endowed in these respects, offered themselves, such as they were, and were found to be admirable pastors and guides of their people. Poverty will always be the lot of the Newfoundland clergy; but to their credit be it said that, spite of this prospect, spite of the frequent perils which attend the exercise of their laborious calling, the priesthood in this poor diocese is threatening to become largely an hereditary one, the clergy desiring nothing better for their sons than that they should be trained in the college at St. John's, which Bishop Feild's forethought provided, to follow them in their steps.

Bishop Feild's episcopate

When Bishop Mountain was consecrated to the

See of Quebec in 1793, there were only six clergymen in Upper and three in Lower Canada, that is to say, in the whole region now divided into the Dioceses of Quebec, Montreal, Toronto, Huron, Ontario, Algoma, and Niagara. The colony, at its cession to England in 1767, numbered only 69,000 souls, and of these only nineteen families did not acknowledge the supremacy of Rome. Immigration and other causes have very much altered this state of things; but to this day, in the diocese of Quebec, out of a population of 560,000, mainly Romanist, only 26,760 are members of the English Church. The cathedral at Quebec was built by George III. in 1804, and the bishop instituted choral worship, importing from England the first organ ever heard in Canada.

<small>The Church in Canada</small>

Bishop Mountain died in 1825, and his successor was one of his own clergy, the Hon. and Rev. Charles James Stewart, who eighteen years previously had volunteered for any post which it was found difficult to fill. He had been sent to St. Armand, on the frontier of the United States, where there was neither church, nor school, nor parsonage, nor religion. Arriving on a Saturday, he put up at an inn, and asked to hire a room for the next day's service. The landlord warned him, not only that no one would come, but that the mere proposal would probably cause a riot. 'Then here is the place for me,' said the brave man, and in that spot he remained, inhabiting one room in a rude farmhouse, for ten years, until the godless settlement had become a Christian parish, with its church and school, and the bishop called him away to another district which demanded his constructive and evangelising

<small>Bishop Stewart</small>

zeal. Two years later he received what he called 'my promotion,' having been appointed travelling missionary of the diocese, a position which he occupied until 1826, when he was called to the episcopate of the diocese in which he had laboured so conspicuously. He lived for ten years in the higher position to which he had been summoned; but the hardships of his priesthood life hindered his efficiency as a bishop. Ill-health drove him to England for medical treatment, and he died in London in 1836. He was succeeded by his coadjutor, Dr. G. J. Mountain, the son of his predecessor.

In 1851 Lower Canada was further subdivided, for ecclesiastical purposes, by the foundation of the See of Montreal. It was the great privilege of Bishop Fulford to inaugurate a system of synodal action, to which the whole Church owes much. He designed and built a handsome cathedral in Montreal, which was consecrated in 1859. No further subdivision of dioceses has yet been made in Lower Canada. The Church is poor, and its members only a small proportion of the population; out of a total of 1,359,027, more than 1,000,000 are Roman Catholics.

Montreal

But in Upper or Western Canada, where a rich soil has attracted emigrants from all parts, the Anglican Church has made more rapid progress. Separated from Quebec by the establishment of the See of Toronto in 1839, it is now divided into the five dioceses of Toronto, Huron, Ontario, Algoma, and Niagara, which occupy the land to the western shores of Lake Superior where the Diocese of Rupert's Land draws its frontier line. In Upper Canada the Indians have been cared for, and, with much success, have been

Upper Canada or the Province of Ontario

induced to settle on the reserves granted to them, and to betake themselves to pastoral habits. Some tribes are still to a great extent Pagan; but the Church of Rome has won a great multitude from heathenism. At Walpole Island and at many other settlements the English pastor is welcomed and recognised as their spiritual guide. The Diocese of Algoma was established in 1873 almost entirely in the interests of the Indians, who live on the shores of Lakes Superior and Huron. The population of 60,000 souls is composed of Indians and poor settlers, the land, except in a few favoured regions, being very unproductive. The first bishop, Dr. Fauquier, a Canadian by birth, died in December 1881, and was succeeded by the Rector of St. George's, Montreal, Dr. Sullivan, who gave up one of the most important churches in Canada for an unendowed missionary diocese. In his steam launch, once the property of H.R.H. the Prince of Wales, and then known as the *Zenobia*, but renamed, on her dedication to the work of the Church, the *Evangeline*, the bishop visits all the settlements on the shores of the lakes. At the Neepigon Mission he found a welcome state of things. An old chief had waited thirty years for the visit of a 'Black Coat,' and although no missionary arrived, on his deathbed he charged his son, 'Wait, he will surely come.' In 1878 the son started to make his wishes known at Toronto, where he met Bishop Fauquier, and the mission was at once established. In four years the whole aspect of the place was changed; the children could read and write, and many also of the adults could read. Log-houses with neatly fenced gardens were substituted for the filthy wigwam, and on all sides signs of civilisation were apparent. In the presence of this progress the bishop expressed his fear that, if immediate steps were not taken to help the colonists to secure for themselves the privileges of religion, while Pagans were being made Christians in one place, Christians would be allowed to lapse into Paganism in others.

In Upper and Lower Canada care has been taken to provide amply for religious teaching. At Lennoxville <small>Education in Canada</small> in the Diocese of Quebec a college and university with staff of professors provides for all the demands of a liberal education. It was founded in 1845, and from its class-rooms have gone forth a regular succession of men qualified to serve God in Church and State. In Upper Canada a theological college, founded in 1842, was subsequently merged in Trinity College. This university owes its origin to the zeal of Bishop Strachan. In 1849 the King's University of Toronto, which had existed for six years and had a hundred students, was by an act of the legislature secularised, and the faculty of theology was suppressed. The bishop, although advanced in years, determined to supply the needs of the Church. 25,000*l*. were raised in Canada, and the bishop visited England and appealed for 10,000*l*., which he readily obtained. From time to time additions were made to the endowments and to the buildings, and in the first thirty years more than 600 graduates, in arts, law, physic, music, or divinity, were trained within its walls. Large schools, in which high education is given to boys and girls, have become affiliated to Trinity College. In 1883 it was found to be necessary to add professorships of mental and moral philosophy, history, English literature, modern languages, and physical science. The university may now be expected, without much fear of disappointment, to confer on Canadians the blessings which Oxford and Cambridge have shed on many generations of Englishmen.

One matter must yet be mentioned, which more than once has involved Canada in strife. By an Act of Parliament passed in 1791, certain lands were reserved 'for the maintenance and support of a Protestant Clergy.' These were mere tracts of snow and forest, and long remained uncultivated. From the end of the American War in 1814 until the Canadian Rebellion of 1838, the Houses of Assembly in both provinces, but especially in Lower Canada, were frequently in collision with the Executive Government. The most fruitful causes of dissension were the rights of the Assembly to control public expenditure and the question of the 'Clergy Reserves.' The immediate exciting cause of the rebellion was the establishment by Sir John Colborne, the governor, of thirty-seven rectories in Upper Canada. After the rebellion was subdued, a new constitution was given to Canada, in which the larger Confederation since adopted was foreshadowed, and in 1840 the Legislature apportioned the lands between the Church of England, the Presbyterians, and some other religious bodies. This did not secure peace; and in 1855 the reserves were applied to municipal purposes, all vested interests being carefully regarded. The Canadian clergy, without exception, commuted their life interests for a capital sum, which was invested for the permanent endowment of the Church.

Deprived of the possessions which had been given to it by the Crown, looking no longer for the patronage of the State, the Church, in 1857, claimed and obtained the right of managing her own affairs through the duly constituted synods of the several dioceses. From that time the Church has rapidly expanded, multiplying her clergy and her dioceses; but the history of the synodal action of the Colonial Churches will be treated in a subsequent chapter.

CHAPTER IV.

THE CHURCH IN NORTH-WEST CANADA.

THE charter, which was given in 1670 by King Charles II. to the Hudson's Bay Company, conferred on that body the possession of a country about the size of the Russian Empire. This was called Rupert's Land, in honour of Prince Rupert, who had founded the company. It extended from the boundary of Western Canada to the Pacific Ocean, and from the frontier of the United States to the Arctic Circle, to the limits, indeed, at which human life can be sustained. There was no scheme of colonisation present to the minds of the early adventurers, and the land was supposed to be poor—an hypothesis which has subsequently been disproved—and, whatever its products, there was no opportunity of reaching the open markets of the world. The whole region was a vast hunting-ground, into which the intrusion of man, beyond the numbers demanded for the prosecution of trade, was not

The Hudson's Bay Company

desired. There was a peculiarity in the settling of this colony, which is not found elsewhere. The Indians were essential to the traders for their work; they were the skilled trappers and huntsmen, and their services were well remunerated. Thus anything like a war of races, which elsewhere has been carried on to the extinction of the aborigines, was not possible. In spiritual things, however, nothing was done for the people during the first 150 years of the company's occupation. The Scottish servants of the company also seem to have dispensed with public worship themselves during that long period; for when the first formal settlement was made under the Earl of Selkirk, at what is now the city of Winnipeg, in 1811, he could find no trace of temple or idol, or place of Christian worship. This settlement, which was distinct from the few forts hitherto erected, was resented by the Indians, who possibly foresaw the advance of the white men and their own extinction. Several forays were made, but peace was re-established. The settlement grew, and in a few years a race of half-breeds, the offspring of Europeans and their Indian wives, became the majority of the population.

The Church Missionary Society, in 1822, sent out two missionaries. The company had two years pre-
<small>Conversion of the Indians</small> viously sent out a chaplain to their own people, the Rev. John West, who opened the way for others. In 1825, the Rev. W. Cochran began a service of conspicuous merit, which lasted for forty years. He was successful in the very difficult work of inducing the Indians to abandon their wandering lives. He literally 'put his hand to the plough,' teaching them

how to use it, to sow, to plant, to reap, to build log houses, and to thatch them. He was the Oberlin of Rupert's Land. As the parents settled, so the children came to school, and of those children he was able, in time, to present one, Henry Budd, for ordination. In 1844, Bishop Mountain of Quebec, being the nearest bishop, made up his mind to pay a visit of inspection to this strange and unknown land. For thirty-two days he sat patiently in open canoes, camping on the ground by night. He did not go beyond the Red River Settlement; but he confirmed 846 persons, ordained one deacon and two priests; and his report of his journey, and the earnest representations which he made, led to the establishment of the Bishopric of Rupert's Land in 1849. In 1818 two Roman priests had settled in Red River, and of these one shortly afterwards was made Bishop of Juliopolis. The Roman Church has well occupied the whole country, and its hierarchy in this province numbers an archbishop and three bishops.

The English bishop, Dr. Anderson, gave himself freely to his work, making long and unaccustomed journeys by canoe and by dog-team, as the season demanded. In 1860 he summoned his clergy to a conference or synod, and some idea of the extent of the diocese is afforded by the fact that two excused themselves from obeying the summons; one was at Fort Simpson, 2,500 miles to the north-west, the other at Moose, 1,200 miles to the east. Bishop Anderson resigned in 1864, and was succeeded by Bishop Machray. The conditions of the country had become changed: immigration had begun, and the English element was increasing, but the country re-

The first English Bishop of Rupert's Land

mained almost in its original isolation. Not quite indeed—originally there had been but two routes to Winnipeg; one by Hudson's Bay, possible only during four months in the year, the other by Canada and the Lakes, which proved so hazardous that it was ultimately abandoned. The development of new States within the United States frontier, Iowa, Minnesota, Dakota, and Nebraska, had opened a new route which brought the bishop to Pembina; but from this point to his future home there stretched a prairie of 600 miles, with no roads except the tracks made by the rough country carts, which were the sole means of locomotion. The bishop compared the settlement, when he at length reached it, to a community of some 10,000 people scattered over an area such as that between Aberdeen and Inverness, with no communications whatever to the northward, and southward with London only by carts over an uninhabited country. This did not last long: the American Railway was carried to San Francisco with extraordinary energy, and ran within 160 miles of the frontier, whence a branch was thrown out. This was considered to be a great achievement, but greater things were yet to come.

<small>Growth of the colony</small>

In 1869, the Hudson's Bay Company, in consideration of a sum of 300,000*l.* with certain reservations of land, surrendered their monopoly of trade and ceded their territorial rights to the Dominion of Canada, which had been established by Royal Proclamation on May 27, 1867, and included the provinces of Ontario, Quebec, New Brunswick, and Nova Scotia. This was not accomplished without some excitement, a

<small>The Canadian Pacific Railway</small>

provisional government, an uprising of the Indians and half-breeds under the famous Riel, and an excellently-planned expedition under Sir Garnet Wolseley. It now appeared that the land which had been supposed to be fit only for the maintenance of the wild animals, that gave to the Hudson's Bay Company their wealth, was the finest wheat-growing country in the world. For 1,000 miles from east to west, where the Rocky Mountains raise their giant ramparts, and for 200 miles from north to south, a virgin soil invites the over-populated countries of the Old World to send their children, with the certainty that they will find competence and even wealth.

A land office was established by the Government in order to minimise the reckless speculation which other colonies have witnessed: 2,000,000 acres were set aside to meet the claims of half-breeds and old residents, and provision was made for education throughout the district. Between 1872 and 1877 inclusive 1,400,000 acres were taken up by immigrants; but this was surpassed in 1878, in which single year 700,000 acres were taken up, and in 1879, when 1,000,000 acres were purchased. No colony has risen with such rapidity. The population of Winnipeg in 1870 was, exclusive of the military, under 300; it is now nearly 30,000. It was, as has been mentioned, a mere hamlet pitched on a vast isolated plain; it is now the centre of a great railway system. The Canadian Pacific Railroad, which was undertaken by the Government with a pledge that it should be completed within ten years, was in 1885 successfully carried throughout the country, and the Pacific shore was reached. This line runs through the fertile wheat-growing belt and connects it with the markets of the world. The Rocky Mountains no longer oppose their impregnable barriers. Westward to China and Japan, and eastward to the Old World, the produce of the newly opened land can be sent with equal facility. It is no longer the Rupert's Land of twenty-five years ago. The seat of government of the North-West Territory has been placed at Regina, which so recently as 1882 had no existence save as part of the far-stretching prairie, but now, 320 miles west of Winnipeg, is raising its buildings and asserting its pre-eminence. Manitoba as a distinct province has its own government. Athabasca, Alberta, Saskatchewan, and Assiniboia are the provinces which make up the North-West Territories of Canada.

It is now time to trace how the spiritual development of this region has kept pace with its material progress. Few positions could be more trying than was that of the Bishop of Rupert's Land when the first sign of the new order of things appeared. There was no time for making preparations; the tide flowed almost without warning, and it knew no ebb. The waste was being cultivated; the immigrants poured in by thousands; whatever their inclinations they had not the means of providing for themselves the rudest church, or any money for the support of their clergy. Neither was there a clerical staff ready to hand, who could follow the immigrants to their clearings, nor was there money wherewith to guarantee to any who might be willing to come to the country even a meagre stipend. In 1872, the north-eastern portion of the diocese became the See of Moosonee, and a man

The development of the Church

who had laboured in that region of frost and snow for twenty years, the Rev. J. Horden, was the first bishop; but his flock were Indians and half-breeds; no colonists would ever be tempted to that barren land. The separation therefore relieved the Bishops of Rupert's Land, but did nothing directly for the incoming settlers. In 1874, the Diocese of Saskatchewan was formed, reaching to the Rocky Mountains, and providing both for the Indians and for the colonists who have subsequently taken up their holdings within its limits. In the same year a diocese, now known as that of Mackenzie River, was established. This again is a diocese for the benefit of the Indians, and the Church Missionary Society's stations have been placed even within the limits of the Arctic Circle. In 1884, two more dioceses were formed, relieving Saskatchewan and Rupert's Land, and are known as the Dioceses of Athabasca and Qu'Appelle. In these southern dioceses the railway mitigates the conditions of isolation which the pioneers in Rupert's Land endured. The Church had a hard struggle at first, and its necessities have been recognised and to some extent met by the Mother Church. The Presbyterians in Canada have helped the members of their communion with much liberality; but the bishops of the north-west complain that their work has not received much help from the older Canadian dioceses. These have suffered in their turn; for the attractions of the newly opened land have drawn from the impoverished soil of older Canada much of the working strength and sinew of its population, and have proportionately weakened the resources of the local Church.

. Popular sentiment does not generally connect

the heroism of missionary life with Canada. It demands in missionary literature a background of waving palms and other tropical vegetation, with incidents of slavery, kidnapping, and the like. Devotion is apt to be measured by the height of the thermometer. It may well be considered whether there be any lives more heroic than those which are passed by the Moravians in Greenland and Labrador, and by the Romanist communities and our own brethren in the Sub-Arctic regions of Northern Canada. They do not obtrude their labours on public notice; they stay at their posts and rarely visit England. They are consequently unknown; and yet what lives they lead! Of educated society they have no share; their people are but the poor Indians and Esquimaux, whose highest energies are given to the snaring of wild beasts and to the catching of fish. For food, only the keen air which gives equally keen appetite will enable a man to keep body and soul together on three meals daily of white fish, the food of the dogs which haul their sleds, which Providence gives in abundance, and which is stored in autumn and allowed to freeze. Luxuries from the outer world can never reach the remote stations on the Athabasca Lake and on the Mackenzie River; numberless portages impede navigation when the rivers are open, and over each of these every pound of freight has to be carried by hand. Tea and flour must be forced into the sterile region, for they are necessaries; but for animal food the missionaries must depend on what the country may produce, and for eight months in the year the white fish is the standing dish. Flowers spring up as if by magic when

Isolation of missionaries in the extreme N.W.

the snow disappears, and simultaneously the heat becomes intense, as the sun continues day and night above the horizon. Then the mosquitos come and bring their irritating hum and piercing stings; but the summer is too short to allow of any vegetable being planted with the hope of its ripening. For communication with the outer world—for books and magazines and letters which come to the missionary in every other part of the world, let the author of 'The Wild North Land' tell the story of the postal arrangements in these latitudes :—

'Towards the middle of the month of December there is unusual bustle in the office of the Hudson's Bay Company at Fort Garry on the Red River; the winter packet is being made ready. Two oblong boxes are filled with letters and papers addressed to nine different districts of the Northern Continent. The limited term 'district' is a singularly inappropriate one; a single instance will suffice. From the post of the Forks of the Athabasca and Clear Water Rivers to the Rocky Mountain Portage is 900 miles, and yet all that distance lies within the limits of the single Athabasca district, and there are others larger still. From Fort Resolution on the Slave River to the rampart on the Upper Yukon, 1,100 miles lay their lengths within the limits of the Mackenzie River district. Just as the days are at their shortest, a dog-sled, bearing the winter packet, starts from Fort Garry; a man walks behind it, another man some distance in advance of the dogs. It holds its way down the Red River to Lake Winnipeg; in about nine days' travel it crosses that lake to the north shore at

Colonel Butler's description of the Mail Service

Norway House; from thence, lessened of its packet for Churchill and the Bay of Hudson, it journeys in twenty days' travel up the Great Saskatchewan River to Carlton. Here it undergoes a complete re-adjustment, and about February 1st it starts on its long journey to the north. During the succeeding months it holds steadily along its northern way, sending off at long, long intervals branch dog-packets to right and left; finally, just as the sunshine of mid-May is beginning to carry a faint whisper of the coming spring to the valleys of the Upper Yukon, the dog-team, last of many, drops the packet, now but a tiny bundle, into the inclosure at La Pierre's House. It has 'travelled nearly 3,000 miles: a score of different dog-teams have hauled it, and it has camped for more than a hundred nights in the great northern forest.'[1]

How the rare infrequent mail is anticipated and watched for, the same author has told us from his own experience in a passage that will well bear quotation:

'I reached the Hudson's Bay Company's Fort of Carlton, the great rendezvous of the winter packets between north and south. From Fort Simpson on the far Mackenzie, from Fort Chipwyan on the lonely Athabasca, from Edmonton on the Upper Saskatchewan, from Isle à la Crosse, dogs had drawn the masters of these remote establishments to the Central Fort. They waited in vain for the arrival of the packet; with singular punctuality had their various teams arrived from starting points 2,000 miles apart; many a time the hillside on which the packet must appear was scanned by watchers, and all the boasted second sight

[1] *The Wild North Land,* by Captain Butler, F.R.G.S.

and conjuring power of haggard squaw and medicine man was set to work to discover the whereabouts of the missing link between the realms of civilisation and savagery. The next morning brought a change. Far away in the hazy drift and "poudre," which hung low upon the surface of the lake, the figures of two men and one sled of dogs became visible. Was it only Antoine Larimgeau, a solitary "freeman" going like a good Christian to his prayers at the French mission? Or was it the much-wished-for packet? It soon declared itself: the dogs were steering for the fort and not for the mission. Larimgeau might be an indifferent Church member, but had the whole college of cardinals been lodged at the fort that Sunday, they must have rejoiced that it was not Larimgeau going to Mass, and that it was the winter packet coming to the fort. What reading we had that day! news from the far-off busy world; letters from the far-off quiet home; glad news and sorry news, borne, through months of toil, 1,500 miles over the winter waste.'

'Where the white man settles the red man disappears.' Sad, indeed, is the saying, which has come almost to rank as an axiom. It is not universally true; for good men, by throwing themselves into the task, have here and there saved aborigines from extinction. As a rule, however, while the hunting-grounds are getting more and more restricted, and the Indians are driven, if they would live, to adopt a mode of life strange and distasteful to them, the race dwindles away while the hard lesson is being learned. Often its decay has been expedited by the whisky cask and the rifle; but in some cases by purely

The Indians

natural causes, the result has been brought about so steadily and without interruption as to appear to be the working of an inevitable law. It has happened in the United States and it will be repeated in Canada. Where the areas are enormous and human and animal life are scattered widely over them, they take long to destroy; 380 years ago, a Portuguese sailor, the forerunner of the hosts of Europeans who have since occupied the land, captured and killed a band of harmless Indians; 360 years ago, a Spanish soldier first saw a herd of buffaloes beyond the valley of the Mississippi. Now the hopeless struggle of the red man and the buffalo, the twin dwellers of the prairie, approaches its end. They are linked together in their lives, and their ends will not be far apart. Indian risings from time to time trouble governments, who point to the reserves which have been provided for the natives; but Indian risings mean the disappearance of the buffalo, the Indian's one friend. Unless his life is altogether changed the Indian cannot do without the buffalo. Its skin gives him a house, its robe a blanket and a bed, its undressed hide covers his boat, its short horn gives a powder-flask; its leather, bit, bridle, and saddle; its inner skin a book on which to record the trophies of his life. Every want, from infancy to age, the buffalo supplies; and after this life, wrapped in his buffalo robe, the red man is laid in his grave, while his spirit joins the heroes of his tribe in hunting-grounds beyond the sun.

The buffalo

British Columbia is the name of the possessions of the Hudson's Bay Company on the western side of the Rocky Mountains. The great barrier, which these interpose, cut it off effectually from intercourse with the regions on the eastern side; and, for the same reasons which operated in Rupert's Land, immigration was not encouraged. The Church Missionary Society sent a missionary to the Indians on the mainland in 1856, and in the following year the Propagation Society sent one to Vancouver's Island. In 1858 the discovery of gold on the Fraser River attracted a large number of Chinese; and for the purpose of maintaining order it was deemed necessary to remove British Columbia from the Hudson's Bay Company and to constitute it a British Colony. The following year saw the consecration of Bishop Hills, the first bishop; a Churchwoman in England having given 15,000*l.* for the endowment of the see, and 10,000*l.* for the endowment of two archdeaconries. Large additional funds were entrusted to the bishop, and he was accompanied by some clergymen of more than average excellence. The work of the Church, however, cannot be said to have fulfilled even moderate expectations. Some of the mines failed, and the population, for whom churches had been built, wandered from place to place or left the colony. The investments which had been made did not realise the interest which had been hoped for; in some cases they paid nothing at all. Some of the clergy returned home, and the missions to the Indians, of which rose-coloured reports gave great hopes, proved to be disappointing. Moreover, the isolation of the colony continued. It could be reached by a long voyage round Cape Horn, from the Isthmus of Panama, or by crossing the American Continent to San Francisco and thence by water. Thus it remained out of the world.

Marginal note: British Columbia

In 1871 it became incorporated in the Dominion of Canada on certain conditions, one, and perhaps the most important, of which was 'the commencement simultaneously, within two years of the date of the union, of the construction of a railway from the Pacific towards the Rocky Mountains, and from such point as may be selected east of the Rocky Mountains towards the Pacific, to connect the sea-board of British Columbia with the railway system of Canada, and further to secure the completion of such railway within ten years from the date of the union.' The railway therefore ought to have been finished in 1881; but, as has been already stated, it was not until the autumn of 1885 that the first train ran through to the Pacific and so fulfilled the contract. In 1879 the diocese was divided, Bishop Hills retained charge of Vancouver's Island and some smaller islands, while the mainland became the two larger dioceses of New Westminster and Caledonia.

Two new dioceses constituted Possibly the immediate result of the opening of the railway will not be an increase of prosperity, as the persons employed on its construction will be withdrawn; but it must shortly influence favourably the condition of the colony. In Caledonia the gold mines on the Cassiar and Stikine Rivers have attracted a large number of adventurers, to whom the bishop has secured the ministrations of the Church; and under circumstances of unusual trial many of the Indian converts have stood by the Church and the bishop. In New Westminster, where missions to the Indians established long ago have given cause for much disappointment, fresh labourers with experience gained in English parishes seem to be making real progress; and the bishop has been fortunate in securing for these missions to a tribe known as the Thompson Indians the services of some sisters from All Saints House at Ditchingham.

CHAPTER V.

THE CHURCH IN THE WEST INDIAN ISLANDS.

THE Church in the West Indian Islands has been from the first a 'state-paid' Church. In the very early years of the seventeenth century the authorities in Barbados enforced conformity and punished with fines each case of non-attendance at church on Sundays. In Jamaica, in the middle of the same century, rectories were established by law and maintained by public funds. The islands generally, but especially Jamaica, which two centuries ago was the chief resort of the buccaneers who infested the Caribbean Sea, have had a troublous history. It was not until 1795 that the last desperate struggle took place between the colonists and the Maroons, who had taken refuge in the mountains. They were deported by Government first to Nova Scotia and ultimately to Sierra Leone. Then the constantly recurring slave rebellions prevented the continuous progress of the islands. In Jamaica there were not fewer than twenty-seven distinct and serious outbreaks between 1678 and 1832. On the last occasion 200 slaves were killed in the field and 500 were executed. The slaves for the most part were kept entirely in ignorance of religion. With the permission of their

[margin: The Church established and maintained by the State]

owners, the clergy were allowed access to them; but their intelligence was dulled by their helpless condition, and they had little time in which to receive instruction.

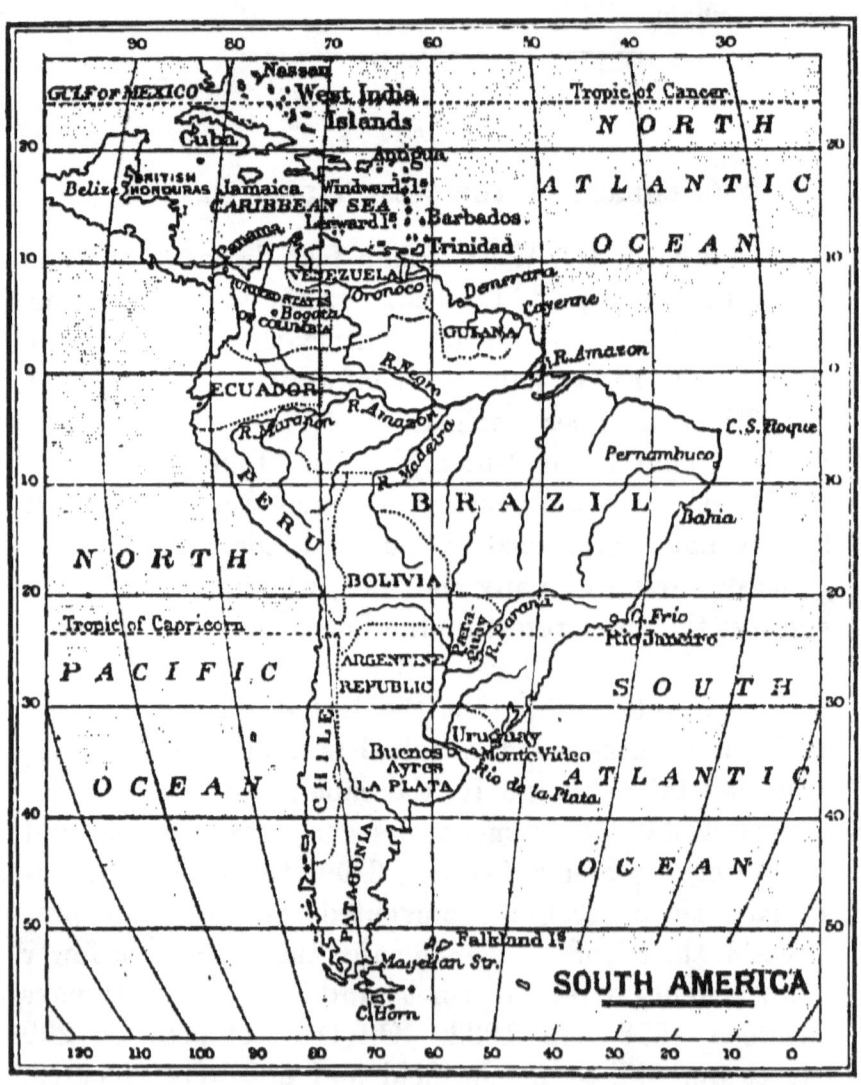

It seems hard to believe that the great Bishop Butler, in 1739, while pleading for their admission to a limited measure of the Church's gifts, should speak of them in the half-hearted words of the following sentence, which occurs in a sermon preached at the anniversary of the Society for the Propagation of the Gospel :

'Of these our colonies the slaves ought to be considered as inferior members, and therefore to be treated as members of them, and not merely as cattle or goods, the property of their masters. Nor can the highest property possible to be acquired in these servants cancel the obligation to take care of their religious instruction. Despicable as they may appear in our eyes, they are the creatures of God, and of the race of mankind for whom Christ died, and it is inexcusable to keep them in ignorance of the end for which they were made, and the means whereby they may become partakers of the general redemption. On the contrary, if the necessity of the case requires that they be treated with the very utmost rigour that humanity will at all permit, as they certainly are, and, for our advantage, made as miserable as they well can be in this present world, this surely heightens our obligation to put them into as advantageous a situation as we are able with regard to another.'

Bishop Butler on slavery

With the emancipation, which came into operation in 1834, a greatly increased desire for religious instruction was everywhere manifested by the freed negroes. To meet this desire a special sum was raised, called the Negro Education Fund. In the next seventeen years the Propagation Society expended 172,000*l.* on this object. In 1840 the Colonial Legislature doubled the number of island curacies in Jamaica, and increased the clerical stipends.

Emancipation

It had been proposed, in the reign of Queen Anne, that bishoprics should be established in Jamaica and Barbados; but it was not until 1824 that the idea was realised, and Bishop Lipscombe was sent to Jamaica, and Bishop Coleridge to Barbados. The Government made most liberal provision, allowing each bishop 3,000*l.* per annum, and allotting stipends on an equally profuse scale to several archdeacons. It was on this occasion that the author of the 'Christian Year' received the only offer of preferment, with the exception of the Vicarage of Hursley, which was ever made to him. Bishop Coleridge wished him to accept the archdeaconry of Barbados. In 1842, on the resignation of Bishop Coleridge, the see was divided into three; and on St. Bartholomew's Day in that year the abbey at Westminster witnessed the consecration of five bishops, for Barbados, Antigua, Guiana, Gibraltar, and Tasmania. In 1861 the Bahamas group were taken from Jamaica, and Archdeacon Caulfield was consecrated first Bishop of Nassau. Thus there were four bishops in the West Indian Islands, and one in Guiana, which had been part of the diocese of Barbados. They were all supported by public funds, as were the large majority of their clergy. The recognition thus given by the State did not secure for the Church an unquestioned supremacy, for the Wesleyans and Baptists wielded very great influence, as their fervid preaching and singing attracted the emotional negroes.

The West-Indian Episcopate

In 1868 a policy of disendowment was forced by the Imperial Government on the several island legislatures. The stipends of the bishops, rectors, and island curates were withdrawn, the vested

Disendowment

interests of their holders being in all cases respected. The blow was a very heavy one, all the more so because it was unexpected. Many of the holders of the grants were old men, and passed away before provision could be made for their successors. The local legislature of Barbados determined to establish a Church in the island for the exclusive benefit of Barbados; and the bishop is maintained by the public moneys of the island, as are also eleven rectors and twenty-seven curates. This law was passed in 1873. In 1878 the other Windward Islands, which are wholly or partially disendowed, were formed into a separate diocese, with their own synods distinct from that of Barbados, and were placed under the charge of the Bishop of Barbados, whose proper title is Bishop of Barbados and the Windward Islands.

The other dioceses have, with assistance from England, raised, and in some instances have completed, endowments for the several bishoprics, as well as funds for the partial endowment of the clergy. The heavy blow of disendowment was not a lasting discouragement. It seemed to draw out a wonderful spirit of self-help; the weekly contributions of the negro flocks of a penny per head are regularly and willingly contributed, and amount to a large sum. In 1872 the island of Trinidad was separated by royal warrant from the Diocese of Barbados, and the Rev. R. Rawle, who had been for more than a quarter of a century Principal of Codrington College, Barbados, was consecrated bishop. In this diocese, the grant to religious denominations, of which the Church of Rome receives the largest share, is being gradually reduced. The Church of England will ultimately receive

Self-help

only 3,000*l.* per annum, instead of 6,325*l.*, which was its share of the total sum in 1870.

Under the supervision of the Bishop of Jamaica is the colony of British Honduras, attached for certain civil purposes to the Government of Jamaica, although possessing its own legislative council. The Church here has its own synod, although its clerical staff has never exceeded three in number. It also is emphatic in proclaiming that it is a distinct and separate diocese, self-contained and self-governed, which has elected the Bishop of Jamaica as its bishop.

British Honduras

The record of Church doings in the West Indies would be very incomplete were no mention made of the noble foundation of General Codrington. Born in Barbados in 1668, educated at Oxford, where he became fellow of All Souls College, in the chapel of which society his body is buried, this good soldier, who had been present at the siege of Namur, bequeathed to the Society for the Propagation of the Gospel two estates in the island for the purpose of maintaining professors and scholars 'who should be obliged to study and practise physic and chirurgery, as well as divinity, that, by the apparent usefulness of the former to all men, they might both endear themselves to the people and have the better opportunities of doing good to men's souls while taking care of their bodies.' The will also stipulated that the Society should for all time keep the plantations entire, and maintain thereon three hundred negroes at the least. On the abolition of slavery the Society received 8,823*l.* 8*s.* 9*d.* as compensation money; but long before the passing of the Act the Society had anticipated the system of

General Codrington's bequest

apprenticeship which was subsequently adopted by the Government. It gave allotments of land to the slaves, who paid rent by their labour on four days in each week; and up to the present time it has maintained a church and chaplain for the labourers, who, in a state of freedom, are its tenants. The Society began to discharge its trust in 1712 by sending out a chaplain and a catechist. The building of a college was commenced; but owing to protracted disputes as to the property it was not completed until 1743, when it was opened, in the first instance, as a grammar school. In 1780 a hurricane laid the building level with the ground, and it was not rebuilt for some years, the property being at that time much depreciated. In 1830, it was opened for the reception of older students, and it now has exhibitions for the benefit of each one of the West Indian dioceses. It has educated a large number of men, some of whom have afterwards attained to distinction in England. More than one hundred and fifty of the West Indian clergy, of whom two have become bishops, have here been trained by successive principals, the first of whom was the Rev. J. H. Pinder, afterwards the first principal of the Theological College at Wells. The college is now affiliated to Durham University, and the students obtain degrees in the several faculties from that university. In 1851, the Church people in Barbados founded an association for furthering the Gospel in Western Africa; the whole of the West Indian dioceses took their part in the work, and the result has been a very chivalrous mission to the Rio Pongas country which will be described in its proper place.

The formation of a Republic in Hayti led to the

establishment of an Anglican Church about the year 1870. The Rev. J. T. Holly, a man of colour, was chosen to be the bishop of this independent Church, and obtained consecration from the Church of the United States, two bishops from America having previously visited the island and held confirmations and ordinations. There are nine priests, five deacons, seventeen lay readers and organised congregations, and twenty mission stations under Bishop Holly's charge.

Hayti and its Church

CHAPTER VI.

THE CHURCH IN SOUTH AMERICA.

THE colony of British Guiana, on the north-east coast of South America, has always been grouped for ecclesiastical purposes with the West Indian Church. It was formerly an archdeaconry of the Diocese of Barbados, and at the present time the Bishop of Guiana is the primate of the West Indian ecclesiastical province. This is now probably the most open missionary field in the world, and its history is of peculiar interest. It was Raleigh's *El Dorado* from which he returned to England to meet imprisonment and death. Portuguese, French, and Dutch, each attempted to colonise it, with uniform failure; and in 1814 the three districts of Demerara, Essequibo, and Berbice were made one British colony. On the slave emancipation in 1834 the Propagation Society first lent a helping hand to the colony. Its help drew forth local effort, and the society was induced to purchase an estate

British Guiana

called 'Hackney,' to be an endowment for a mission among the aborigines on the Pomeroon River, which has developed into a vast work, of which more will be said hereafter. The Moravians laboured for seventy years among the negroes in the Berbice; but they have long retired from the colony. The Church Missionary Society laboured from 1831 till 1853 among the Indians in the Essequibo, but at the latter date the missionaries of that society were withdrawn.

The English colonists and the negroes have all along been cared for in religious matters by the State, the Church, in common with other bodies, receiving grants from public funds, according to their respective numbers of members. The missionary work has been carried on with very remarkable success among (1) the Indian aborigines, (2) the coolies imported from India and China.

<small>Evangelistic work</small>

(1) Bishop Coleridge in 1827, the year after the addition, by letters patent, of the colony to his spiritual charge, visited the Pomeroon and became acquainted with the tribes of aborigines who peopled the vast savannahs and forests of the interior. Three missions were commenced, and in 1840 the Propagation Society sent out a young layman, Mr. W. H. Brett, who was stationed on the Pomeroon River some forty-five miles from its mouth. Here was a small strip of cleared land, with three rude huts which had been built by a gang of negro woodcutters who had gone off, on the expiration of their apprenticeship in 1838, to join their brethren in the towns. There was also a dilapidated wooden building which had been used for worship on the infrequent occasion of an itinerant

<small>The Indian tribes</small>

clergyman or catechist visiting the river. This was to be the future chapel of the mission. One of the huts was occupied by an old white man, sick with fever and ague; another was the abode of an old negress who had several children living with her; the third was appropriated by Mr. Brett. The river, when flooded by tropical rains, penetrated the floor; the leaky roof with its rotten thatch afforded little protection; and tiger-cats and frogs were numerous and annoying. For his food Mr. Brett was dependent on the Indians, and without their canoes he could not move about. The Indians despised his youth, having an excessive veneration for old age; the sorcerers, finding their craft in danger, threatened his life. He began a small school for the negroes, hoping thereby to attract the Indians; the exact contrary was the result, for there was no community of feeling between the two races, but a strong antipathy. Fever, which frequently seized on him, was a great discouragement, but he manfully persevered. A solitary Indian, who had been absent from his people for some time, presented himself one day at the door of Mr. Brett's cottage. He had seen the work of missionaries on the Essequibo, and, without any direct instruction, had thrown away the instruments of magic which had been his stock-in-trade as a sorcerer, yet for himself he did not seek Christianity. He wished his children to be instructed, and promised to return. This he did, with wife and children and several relatives, and the school was soon filled. The day had dawned and the clouds had rolled away. The Indian, Saccibarri (Beautiful Hair), was christened Cornelius, and through the rest of his life he remained true to the Church, and on his deathbed charged his sons to continue the pious labours which for twenty-eight years had been to himself labours of love. With the conversion of Cornelius the Arawak tribe were soon won over. The chief at once promised his friendship, and the conversion of the tribe was only a work of time. In 1843 the bishop visited the Mission, confirmed and admitted to communion forty natives, and ordained Mr. Brett. The Arawaks are the most numerous of the tribes, and their settlements lie in an extended line within 100 miles of the sea. Next to them come the Waraws, and behind them the Caribs. Another tribe, the Accawoios, are migratory in their habits. Mr. Brett, who all along had been studying the various languages in the hope of reducing them to system, now turned his attention to the Waraws. They trusted him, and admitted that the Gospel was good for the Arawaks but not for themselves. Just as Mr. Brett was in despair, he heard from a catechist at the mouth of the river that some Waraws had attended his services there. Thus encouraged, he opened a mission for these people. As he set out on his expedition, the Arawaks who had been at church the day before, standing on the banks and waving their hands, bade him God-speed. This mission penetrated the country of the Waraws and next reached the Caribs, till Mr. Brett found himself at last in the country of the Accawoios, who had the reputation of being treacherous thieves, adepts in the art of poisoning.

The work was carried on year by year with much patience and amid many discouragements. More than once Mr. Brett's health failed and he had to leave for a time. Smallpox visited the settlements and the scourge was declared by the sorcerers to be the revenge of the Deity on the people for embracing Christianity; a pseudo-Christ appeared and claimed the allegiance of the tribes. On the other hand, these troubles humbled the people, and other labourers came to Mr. Brett's assistance. In 1851 more than 1,000 Indians had been baptized; and on the occasion of the bishop's visit, members of the tribes, which for generations had never met without indulging in all the cruelties of Indian warfare, knelt side by side in fullest amity to receive the Holy Communion. The Indians from the inland regions were drawn to the mission and voluntarily sought to be instructed. In 1868 the Bishop of Guiana went up to the Great Falls of the Demerara river, and on his arrival found that the Indians, who had carried their canoes to the foot of the rapids, had formed an encampment while awaiting his arrival. It was a scene worthy of the earlier ages of the Church; there, in the primæval forest, were the Pagans seeking baptism. Three hundred and ninety-six persons were baptized during the bishop's stay. The chief, wishing no longer to live beyond the reach of instruction, cleared a settlement near the scene of his baptism and built a school and chapel. A catechist remained behind, and ten months later the archdeacon visited the spot and baptized seventy-nine. Altogether 535 persons had been baptized, where, two years before, the Gospel had never reached. The Accawoios, being the pedlars of the land, carried with them everywhere the news of the mission. Mr. Brett's translations brought the Scriptures and Collects within the reach of all. From the Potaro and other rivers in the country various tribes sent their embassies to inquire and report, until in 1874 the Government became so convinced of the advantages afforded by the establishment of mission stations among the Indians that it provided stipends for missionary curates on the Pomeroon and Essequibo rivers. Thus, in the lifetime of one man and very largely by his individual effort, many tribes of Indians have been won from savagery and superstition to civilisation and Christianity.

(2) After the emancipation of the negroes it was found necessary to supplement their uncertain and independent labour by a system of immigration.

The Coolies

In 1845 this was commenced under legal provisions, and within twelve months 10,000 coolies had arrived from India and China. They brought with them all their heathen superstitions, and insisted on publicly performing their heathen ceremonies, some of which would have been forbidden in India. Their processions generally halted in front of Christian churches, and the excitable negroes would follow and applaud as loudly as the Hindoos themselves. One of the clergy wrote that he had seen the Hindoos suspend their votaries, by hooks driven into their backs below the ribs, from a circular swing forty feet above the ground, keeping them constantly in a revolving motion for ten minutes, amid shouting and drum-beating, the Creoles looking on and enjoying the sight. In the first four years 120,000 coolies had arrived. The clergy could do nothing amid the babel of tongues; but missionaries who could speak to them in their own languages were brought from India, and partly supported by the Government. It was then found that they were very open to Christian instruction, and the

Hindoo Christians of the colony are now an important factor in the Church. Even more remarkable has been the work among the Chinese, of whom some 15,000 coolies have been received. The bishop declares that among them are characters 'which have recalled to mind vividly the stories of the early converts to the religion of the Cross.' These coolies are under indentures which bind them for five years, after which they are free to return to their native countries. It is obvious, therefore, that they may be made unconscious evangelists to their kindred; and this has happened, for the clergy in China have on many occasions written to Guiana in the highest terms of the witness which the returned coolies have borne to the religion which they had embraced during their years of exile.

At the southern extremity of the South American Continent the Falkland Islands give a title and a home to an English bishop, whose chief work is among the Patagonians on the mainland. The mission owes its existence to the persistent but eccentric energy of Captain Allen Gardiner, who, after several attempts to establish missions in Natal, came to England and founded an association for the conversion of the Indian tribes of South America. Thrice did he lead expeditions to Patagonia in 1845, 1848, and 1850. The third was fatal to the whole party. They endured many hardships, both from the climate and from the treachery of the natives, while seeking for a site on which to build a house. At length, one after another, the whole of the gallant little band died of starvation; and when a ship of war afterwards touched at Picton Island to inquire into the fate of the

The Falkland Islands and Patagonia

mission the sad tragedy was revealed. On the ruins of this venture a society was formed which is known as the South American Missionary Society. In 1857 a son of Captain Gardiner landed on the coast where his father had died. He knew of two persons who were likely to be of use, one a native who had been brought into contact with Englishmen and had even visited England, the other a Danish layman, who for a year had lived with the natives, sharing their tents and their food and moving with them in their wanderings. The mission has been doing its work for nearly thirty years. Stations have been formed at Keppel, one of the Falkland Islands, and at Ushuwīa on Tierra del Fuego; and a schooner called after the founder of the mission, keeps the various workers in communication. The bishop has also charge of the various English chaplaincies on the eastern and western coasts of South America, which, originally connected with the Foreign Office and maintained by public funds, are now thrown on the resources of the respective congregations.

CHAPTER VII.

THE CHURCH IN AUSTRALIA.

THE loss of the American colonies in 1783 seemed to English statesmen to have landed their country on the verge of ruin, and on the continent England was considered to have been effaced from the list of European States. But the calamity, if for a time it checked the prosperity of England, immediately established the supremacy of the English race. In 1783 there was a population of three millions in the American States clinging to the coast-line of the Atlantic; now there are more than forty millions of people covering the land from the Atlantic to the Pacific. The greatness of England, which is inseparably connected with that of the peoples who speak her tongue, has in the last hundred years flowed

Loss of the American Colonies redressed by the discovery of New Holland

forth, not in one, but in two ever-deepening and widening streams. If trade has not found its chief centres only on the banks of the Mersey and the Thames, but also on the Hudson and the Mississippi, its growth and development generally in this period have been almost as the product of a magician's wand.

The times were in all respects favourable; for, simultaneously with the loss and discouragement in America, there was dawning an era of unparalleled manufacturing energy and scientific discovery at home. Moreover, loss of territory in one part of the world was to be more than atoned for by the discovery of new lands in another. In 1770 Captain Cook had discovered New Holland. The value of the possession was unknown, as were also the extent and the capacities of the country. Statesmen had not been quick to colonise it; but in 1787 the attempt had to be made. The future of the Australian continent had not been conceived; it served only to relieve an immediate difficulty. With America closed, the Government knew not how to dispose of the criminal population. The prisons and penitentiaries, exceptionally crowded and pestilential as they were, were serving the philanthropic John Howard with arguments for enforcing his indictment against their moral condition. Therefore in May 1787, just three months before the consecration of the first colonial bishop, the first convict ships were sent to Botany Bay. The fleet consisted of six vessels, accompanied by the 'Sirius' frigate and the 'Supply,' an armed tender. Two hundred soldiers were sent with them to keep discipline, and to suppress any signs of mutiny; but clergyman, schoolmaster, anyone to speak of religion and of reformation —these the Government did not think necessary. How had the national spirit declined! Where were the

<small>Captain Cook</small>

<small>Convict settlements</small>

successors of 'Master Wolfall' and Robert Hunt? Where was the spirit of Raleigh, of Frobisher, of Baltimore, of Nicholas Ferrar, of Robert Boyle? Just at the last moment a clergyman was permitted, on the representation of the Bishop of London, to join the emigrants, without pay and without the prospect of pay. The voyage lasted eight months and one week, including a detention at Rio de Janeiro. In this harbour the good chaplain visited all the ships in turn, while at sea his ministrations benefited only his immediate fellow-passengers.

On arrival, Botany Bay was found to be unsuitable for a settlement, on several grounds, but notably because there was an insufficient supply of water. Proceeding along the coast, the ships came to a spot marked in Cook's chart as a 'boat harbour,' called, after the sailor who first discovered it, *Port Jackson*. Here was a harbour large enough to contain the whole of the navy, navigable for men-of-war for fifteen miles from its mouth, and sheltered from all winds. Here, then, was the first settlement pitched; the thick woods were for the first time made to sound with the woodman's axe, and the kangaroos, as numerous as rabbits in a warren, scuttled away from the presence of the new possessors.

<small>Port Jackson occupied</small>

The formal settlement was not made without some ceremonial; not indeed of the kind which consecrated the early settlement of Virginia, when Eucharist and solemn prayers seemed to the adventurers of the sixteenth century the appropriate commencement of their undertaking. On January 28, 1788, the flag of England was run up; salutes were

<small>Ceremonies observed</small>

fired and rations of spirits were served out to the soldiers and convicts with which to drink to the health of King George III., as the foundations were laid of what is now the fair city of Sydney, with its 240,000 souls. Neither was it thought necessary, while barracks, prisons, and official residences were being built, to set apart any building as a church. Mr. Johnson, the solitary chaplain, held service in the open air wherever he could find a shady spot, till after six years he built a church at a cost of 40*l*. of his own means. It was soon burned down by the convicts, who in three years had increased to the number of 3,500. Their numbers threatened a famine, as some ships which had been despatched with stores had been delayed; their fears urged them to rebellion, and discipline was made even more stringent. Stone churches were now ordered to be built, more as a punishment to the prisoners, who had thought to escape the infliction of church-going, than for any benefit intended to their souls. The prisoners were marched to church as to a roll-call, the officials of the colony attending only when duty compelled them. Among the convicts was a Roman priest, who received a conditional pardon in order that he might exercise his clerical functions in Sydney, Parramatta, and Hawksbury. In 1794, Mr. Johnson was joined by the Rev. S. Marsden, who will be known for all time in connection with the earlier history of New Zealand. In the following year the Propagation Society commenced a work in Australia which has been continued for ninety years at a total expenditure of more than a quarter of a million of money. In 1817, the Government appointed five chaplains to minister to a population of 17,000 souls, of whom 7,000 were convicts. In 1833, this population had increased to 61,000, including 18,000 convicts, who, with the masters to whom they had been assigned, were gradually developing the resources of the land. Free emigration had followed upon the system of transportation, and the condition of the colony at length forced itself on public attention. 'They must have a Church,' said the Duke of Wellington in 1829; and he selected the Rev. W. G. Broughton, curate of Farnham, who had come under his notice at Strathfieldsaye, as archdeacon of New South Wales, which by the fiction of letters patent formed a part of the diocese of Calcutta. What was the extent of this archdeaconry its holder described a quarter of a century later, when speaking in Hertfordshire; he said: 'Imagine your own archdeacon having one church at St. Albans, another in Denmark, another at Constantinople, while the bishop should be at Calcutta—hardly more distant from England than from many parts of the Archdeaconry of Australia.' During the first five years of his residence, he travelled incessantly over the country —then so little known and so sparsely peopled—and he returned to England to lay before the Church the gigantic nature of the task which was imposed on it. At the same time the testimony of an excellent judge, Sir W. Burton, who knew all the evils of the system which had prevailed in Australia, startled public sentiment and received the attention of Parliament.

<small>Free Immigrants</small>

In 1836, Archdeacon Broughton was consecrated first Bishop of Australia, and he returned, with his burdens indeed increased, but with his hands strengthened. He had a seat on the Legislative Council, and in that position he exercised great influence in the determination of educational and other social questions. He held a service at a small township where, three years before, the Yarra Yarra was flowing in uninterrupted solitude. This was Melbourne in 1838; no clergyman knew it, but an excellent layman read prayers and a sermon every Sunday. The next year a clergyman was appointed, and in the year following, so rapidly did the place grow in prosperity, a church was ordered to be built at a cost of 7,000*l.*

First Australian Bishop

Melbourne in 1838

He visited South Australia, and in county after county he found neither church nor worship. He visited also Tasmania, which was not included in his letters patent, and New Zealand, which had not yet become a British colony. In 1842 he had the happiness of seeing a bishop appointed to Tasmania, and in the previous year Bishop Selwyn had been consecrated Bishop of New Zealand. But these hardly relieved Bishop Broughton of his personal responsibility; in 1847 he was able to secure, by a sacrifice of one fourth of his own income, the consecration of three bishops for Newcastle, Adelaide, and Melbourne. These sees have again been divided, and the Australian episcopate now has thirteen bishops, but the history of the whole colony may be taken as that of the four dioceses which, in 1847, nominally, at least, covered the whole continent.

New Zealand and Tasmania

Growth of the Episcopate in Australia

The first Bishop of Newcastle (Tyrrell) is famous, among other things, for having resolutely remained at his post. He is known as 'the one bishop who never came home.' From his arrival in 1848 until his death in 1879, he never left Australia

Newcastle

except to make a voyage of inspection and evangelisation, in company with Bishop Selwyn, in the Melanesian group. He lived in the saddle, making visitation tours of 1,500 miles at a time. His great diocese had 800 miles of coast-line, extended inland 700 miles, and was five times as large as Great Britain. With very high spiritual gifts, he had the rare combination of excellent habits of business. He was a great financier; setting a munificent example, he induced the colonists to give largely. He inaugurated an endowment scheme of 100,000*l.*, taking care that no parish should possess a sum that would provide the full stipend of its clergy, for that, he said, 'would not be a healthy state of things'; but by a combination of partial endowments and the voluntary system, he maintained the advantages and avoided the evils of both. His own property he carefully invested, and it prospered wonderfully. He had always intended to bequeath it to his diocese; and by his will he crowned the edifice of his scheme by providing a magnificent endowment, which, on the return of more prosperous times, will probably be worth 250,000*l.* Nor was this secured by parsimonious hoarding; on the contrary, his gifts in his lifetime were on a lavish scale. In 1859, he contributed largely to the endowment of the See of Brisbane, which relieved him of the charge of the portion of Queensland which had hitherto been under his charge, extending from the 29th to the 22nd parallel of South latitude. This diocese received its third bishop (Webber) in 1885, Bishops Tufnell and Hale having retired in 1874 and 1884 respectively. In 1867, not without Bishop Tyrrell's liberal help, the See of Grafton and Armidale

Diocese of Brisbane

was formed, a large portion of the endowment having been contributed by a lay colonist. The first bishop (Sawyer) had not long begun his work when he was drowned in the Clarence River. His successor (Turner) was consecrated in 1869.

<small>Grafton and Armidale</small>

The huge Diocese of Sydney, long ere this date, had been divided yet further. The discovery of gold had brought to New South Wales and to Victoria a horde of adventurers, for whom the Church was bound to care, although as a rule they were not forward to contribute much of their gains for the support of religion. The unique occasion drew out a man of special qualifications for the work. The Rev. E. Synge was maintained by the Propagation Society, while, as travelling chaplain to the Bishop of Sydney, he made enormous journeys over the outlying regions which had not yet been included in any of the newly formed dioceses. Day after day he rode over the open plains, steering his way by compass, with kangaroos and emus for the companions of his solitude, to find at nightfall a lodging either in a woolshed, where he would hold service for people who had long been estranged from religion, or in the shanties and tents of the diggers, who were amazed at finding a fellow-creature indifferent to the passion which possessed themselves, and seeking only their good. One result of his labours was the formation in 1863 of the Diocese of Goulburn, to the endowment of which a single colonial family contributed 5,000*l*. In 1869, this new see was divided, and the Diocese of Bathurst was formed, a grandson of Samuel Marsden, the Apostle of New Zealand, being the first bishop; and in 1884, by a

<small>The Church and the gold-diggers</small>

<small>Dioceses of Goulburn, Bathurst</small>

munificent gift of 10,000*l.* made by a colonist, the Hon. John Campbell, portions of the two dioceses were united into the new See of Riverina, to which the Rev. Sydney Linton was consecrated. Another act of colonial liberality has to be chronicled. A Sydney layman founded a theological college at Liverpool, twenty miles from the capital, which is known as Moore College, after the name of its founder.

and Riverina

In Melbourne the gold fever and reckless speculation in land, with its inevitable reaction, had a bad effect on the development of the Colony in its earlier years. The city sprang up like a gourd, land and wages and food were at famine prices; but soon the labour market was glutted, land became a drug and a sheep fetched 1*s.* 6*d.* Then the gold-fields gave a prosperity so brilliant as to be a doubtful gain. State aid was given to religious bodies, and was withdrawn in 1875. The material progress of the Church has kept even pace with that of the colony. In 1851 there were only five churches and four parsonages. In 1885 there were in the two dioceses of Melbourne and Ballaarat, which last-named see was established in 1875, 149 parishes and 143 clergymen. Bishop Moorhouse, who succeeded Bishop Perry at Melbourne in 1876, was successful in at once inciting the colony to do more for Church work. Large funds were speedily raised for the erection of a cathedral. Scholarships were founded at Trinity College, Melbourne. Church Congresses, which are of very recent date in England, were introduced by the bishop into the Southern Hemisphere, and he also secured visits from England of clergymen experienced in the conduct of parochial missions for the building up of the spiritual life of the people. The translation of such a man to the important see of Manchester in 1886 was an act as much to the interest of the Mother as it was to the loss of the Daughter Church.

In the Diocese of Adelaide Bishop Short found that, alone of the Australian prelates, he had the task of organising the Church wholly without State aid. One of the first acts of the newly constituted legislature of the colony was to abolish all expenditure of public moneys for religious purposes. It has from the first been in the main a pastoral colony with a yeoman population, and its career has not been subjected to the vicissitudes which have characterised Victoria and New South Wales. Two acres of land given to the Church by an early colonist have proved of enormous value, as in the growth of the city they became a part of its very centre of wealth and business. When Bishop Short, in his eightieth year, retired from his diocese in 1881 he left to his successor a noble cathedral, an episcopal residence, a theological college, St. Peter's Collegiate School and Chapel with fifty-five acres of ground, and a diocesan office in which the Church Synod meets and the organisation of the diocese finds its head quarters. He left also a diocese much smaller in area than he found it; for in 1857 the western portion, coterminous with the colony of Western Australia, had become a separate diocese under the charge of Bishop Hale. This was, and continues to be, from a combination of circumstances, the least progressive of the Australian dioceses. It has, however, been conspicuous for care bestowed on the native races, of whom more will be said hereafter.

Tasmania, the Australian Isle of Wight, favoured by an exceptional climate, has attracted a superior class of colonists and may be regarded as one of the choicest portions of the Queen's dominions. A body of fifty-six clergy welcomed their new bishop, Dr. Sandford, in 1883; and the Tasmanian Church is flourishing and well able to care for all its needs.

<small>Tasmania</small>

In spite of the rapid subdivision of the Australian dioceses, there remained until 1878 an enormous territory extending over eleven degrees of latitude, which, according to the tenor of the letters patent, still remained under the charge of the Bishop of Sydney. Three dioceses, indeed, lay between the metropolitical city and these distant regions, but the bishops had their hands full. Into this country, with its fertile soil and tropical climate, capital flowed and developed new forms of industry. The squatters of North Queensland are not only breeders of sheep, oxen, and horses; they grow sugar, coffee, and other products of tropical climes, according to the elevation of their several holdings. The Queensland Immigration Acts have had to be supplemented by legislation providing for the Chinese and Polynesian labourers who were essential to the successful operations of these colonists.

<small>North Queensland</small>

In 1871 the late Bishop of Sydney was convinced of the necessity of making North Queensland an independent diocese, but not until 1878 was Dr. Stanton consecrated. He went, as he said, expecting to find log-huts and wigwams, and he beheld well-built houses and large towns. He feared that he should meet with irreligion and indifference, and he was welcomed with enthusiasm and affection. He went with a stipend guaranteed to him from England, and he has in an incredibly short time, within seven years, completed an endowment of 15,000*l.* for the see and an endowment for the clergy of 5,000*l.* well invested in land and mortgages. Finding four ugly churches, he insisted on chancels and proper appointments with which to teach the alphabet of worship to those who were ignorant of it. In seven years every township had two churches, while travelling clergymen, whose lives were passed in the saddle, cared for the people widely scattered in the bush and on distant 'runs.'

Thus in fifty years one diocese has become thirteen, and these are compacted together by a perfect system of diocesan and provincial synods, duly recognised by the legislature as corporations with perpetual succession, in which bishops, priests, and laity have each their part conducing to the smooth and efficient working of the whole machine.

<small>Summary</small>

Few more splendid positions—whether regard be had to the influence which a natural leader of men possesses among his fellows, or to the future of the Church of this magnificent continent—are to be found than is the office to which, with the enthusiastic approval of both England and Australia, Canon Barry was called in 1884. He, indeed, reaped where others had sown. Instead of the solitary clergyman who in 1787 volunteered for the task of ministering to a convict flock, who cared little for his labours, he found 575 clergymen ministering to a population of more than three millions, and the Church no longer an exotic but rooted in the soil and managing her own concerns. But this development marked a new point of departure and

<small>Bishop Barry</small>

emphasised the demand for a leader of consummate gifts equal to the changed condition of the Church. These colonies are probably on the eve of forming a confederation, analogous with that which already prevails in the Dominion of Canada, which will bind them together in plans for the common advancement and at the same time will solve the jealousies which are wont to spring up in separate but contiguous colonies. The wisdom of the scheme has commended itself to the world; and it may be permitted to the Church to feel some satisfaction that in this matter she has taken the lead and has set the example of Christian confederation with the happiest results to herself and to the benefit of her children.

To this picture of growth and prosperity there is a dark side, a chapter in the unwritten history of Australian colonisation. Little mention has yet been made of the Aborigines of Australia; but they must not be passed over, nor is the record wholly discreditable. In Tasmania they have long disappeared. After many years of persecution at the hands of the white man the miserable remnant of the race that once owned the soil were gathered together, some by capture, some by persuasion, and were transported to Flinders Island in Bass's Straits. The last capture was made in 1842, the year of the consecration of the first bishop. In spite of the provisions made for what, from the white man's view, were their comforts, the race declined. In 1847 the survivors were moved to Oyster Cove, where twenty years later the last survivor died. On the mainland the case has been different. In the early days of the colony every cruelty and every crime were freely resorted to in the hope of extirpating

Aborigines and their treatment

the race. The white man showed himself to be a savage when removed from the restraints of public opinion and beyond the reach of the law. Poison as well as the bullet was freely used; 'fire-water,' less rapid but hardly less sure in its results, was introduced among the natives with a view to their extermination. But of the crimes of bygone times it is not worth while to write. Can the savage be civilised and converted to Christian habits and to the practice of a life of devotion? This is the problem, which it must be confessed the Australian Church has been slow to solve. Yet have attempts been made, and never without success. First in point of time and in other ways must be mentioned the interesting work of the first Bishop of Adelaide, Bishop Short. This was at Poonindie, near Port Lincoln; here he obtained from the Government an extensive 'run' on which sheep and cattle were bred. Thus the natives were provided with work of a kind that was not novel to them, and gradually were led to adopt civilised and Christian customs. They were paid for their labour and encouraged in thrift. Service was held every day in the Station Church, at which the voluntary attendance was singularly large. The school became famous for athleticism, and a native eleven won a match against St. Peter's College in the city of Adelaide. The man who had devoted himself to the work of this institution became in 1857 the first Bishop of Perth. Here Dr. Hale found his experience of much service. There were 2,000 natives settled in the colony, while the wandering tribes roamed over the land in numbers that could not be estimated with any degree of accuracy. A

Poonindie Institution

small institution for natives had been founded at Albany and had struggled for years against the prejudices of the colonists. At length an officer who had retired from the army, and his like-minded wife, determined to give themselves up to the work of the institution. The governor was induced to visit and examine the various departments of the work, with the result that the Government placed it on a footing of permanent usefulness as an institution of the colony. Other institutions of a similar kind have since been formed, notably in the diocese of Goulburn. Here a clergyman, holding an important charge, became more and more impressed by the guilty neglect of the blacks. In time his indignation gave place to enthusiasm, and as no one would undertake the work he determined to go himself. He had but little money and that was soon spent; but at the darkest hours he had signs of encouragement, and in time he had obtained a run of 2,100 acres, on which he had a farm and schools and a Christian village known as Warangesda. The intelligence of the black children is very high; the schools have obtained from the Government the largest grant that is possible, and to these has now been added a training college from which it is intended to send forth a succession of teachers who will carry the Gospel to the survivors of the Australian tribes. How many in number these may be is not known. They exist in considerable force in the northern districts reaching up to Cape York and the Gulf of Carpentaria. In the extreme north alone they are supposed to number 50,000, and at present to show no signs of a decaying race. There may therefore yet be a 'native church' of Australia. Neither are the obligations of the Australian

Church limited to the native pagans. The demands of commerce are daily bringing to Australia Polynesians speaking a babel of languages, and Chinese coolies. For these some provision has been made, especially in Queensland where the bulk of the coolie labour is found. The time has come too when the church of this continent must look further afield. It has, indeed, assisted with money the Melanesian mission ever since 1850, when the six bishops of the Pacific met at Sydney and established a Board of Missions in the interests of the Melanesian group. But that mission has looked mainly to New Zealand for government and to England for funds.

It seems likely that Australia will annex for civil purposes the whole or a part of the large island of New Guinea. It has been touched by Presbyterian mis-
New Guinea sionaries who have reached it from the adjoining islands, which have been the chief scenes of their very excellent work. The civil annexation will compel the Australian Church to complete the spiritual annexation of an island, worthy almost of the name of continent, which will form a connecting link between itself and the missions in Borneo and the Straits.

CHAPTER VIII.

THE CHURCH IN NEW ZEALAND.

A FEW unsavoury savages hanging about a small colonial town called Paramatta in New South Wales, and there, in 1806, being noticed by the Rev. Samuel Marsden, the second clergyman who had ever landed in Australia—this is the first link of a series, of which the last is a civilised and Christian nation, keen in the maintenance of their Church and its discipline, and giving their own sons to the work of the ministry. The reputation of these Maoris had preceded them to Australia; they were known to be savages and cannibals. Captain Cook had visited New Zealand and had observed that the people were always engaged in intertribal wars. In 1772 twenty-eight men had been cut off from a French ship and massacred. In 1782 ten sailors were seized and eaten in triumph. In 1809, three years after Samuel Marsden had opened communication with the Maoris, the whole crew of H.M.S. 'Boyd' were murdered. Soon after this event a native chief named Tippahee became the guest of Marsden, who learned from him much concerning his people. They were not without a religion, but they had neither hereditary priesthood nor prescribed acts of worship. They worshipped a supernatural power whom they called 'Atua,' and there were many inferior Atuas, including the spirits of their departed ancestors. These they consulted in times of difficulty, and the oracle was wont to reply in a mysterious sound, 'half whisper, half whistle.' Every child was, from the moment of its birth, regarded as holy and to be handled only by the initiated. Nevertheless it was carried to a priest, who, among other ceremonies, recited a long list of names of its ancestors, from which one was at last selected. As this was pronounced the child was solemnly sprinkled with a small branch of a native shrub. In some parts of the island the ceremony was

NEW ZEALAND AND PACIFIC

performed in a running stream, and the child was sometimes immersed in the water. The neophyte was then dedicated to the God of War, and petitions were offered that he might 'flame with anger and be strong to wield a weapon.' The Maoris had also the religious system of 'Tapu,' which prevails over sixty degrees of latitude in the Pacific, and has under another name made itself felt as a heavy religious burden in Madagascar.

On the representation of Mr. Marsden, the Church Missionary Society determined, in 1809, to send a mission to New Zealand; and the first party, consisting of a schoolmaster, a carpenter, and a shoemaker, were sent out to Australia, where Marsden was to meet them. In that year the massacre of the crew of the 'Boyd' had occurred; and it was not until 1814 that the little party, accompanied by Duaterra, the nephew of Tippahee, landed in the northern island. It happened that the spot on which they landed was the scene of the recent murder; but in Duaterra they had an interpreter. On the night of December 20, 1814, Marsden slept in safety on New Zealand soil, the natives lying around with their spears' heads buried in the ground in proof of their friendship. On Christmas Day, the very same day on which, by a curious coincidence, Bishop Middleton preached his first sermon in Calcutta, Marsden commenced his mission by preaching to the people, Duaterra being his interpreter, on the words 'Behold, I bring you glad tidings.' But the time of success was slow in coming. The teachers were protected, even patronised; but their teaching was not valued. In 1820 a chief named Hongi, by his own desire, visited England. He spent some time at Cam-

[margin: First Mission to New Zealand]

bridge, where Professor Lee was enabled to reduce the Maori language to grammar, and so to provide for the people's instruction in reading and writing. The chief had an interview with George IV., who gave him the doubtful present of a supply of fire-arms. Returning to his native land he determined not only to give to it the blessings of the monarchy, but to be himself the monarch. He therefore challenged the neighbouring chief, and, with the present of the English sovereign, gained an easy victory. He drank the blood of his murdered foe and devoured his eyes, while his followers killed and ate as many of his people as they listed, and enslaved the rest. This was seven years after Marsden's landing, and was the conduct of a man who, though not professing Christianity, had faithfully protected the missionaries.

Years went on and no converts were made. The mission staff was increased. In 1822 the Rev. H. Williams, and in 1825, the Rev. W. Williams, afterwards Bishop of Waiapu, landed in New Zealand and commenced the work which ended only with their lives. In 1825 the first conversion was made; but five more years elapsed before any further baptisms were recorded. Meanwhile English settlers were increasing and frequent affrays reduced the numbers of the natives; but in spite of this the progress of the Gospel now became very rapid. The Maoris consulted their 'Atuas' whether the white man's teaching was true, and, strange to say, in every case the answer was in the affirmative. The whole of the New Testament and Prayer Book was translated and printed in 1838. In that year Bishop Broughton visited the islands

First results

and inspected the missions. Two years later, by the wish of the natives, the treaty of Waitangi transferred to England the sovereignty of the islands, the land remaining in the possession of the people. An English Company had already bought large tracts of land and had built the towns of Wellington and Nelson. In 1841 Bishop Selwyn was consecrated the first bishop of New Zealand, and on his landing he wrote, 'We see here a whole nation of Pagans converted to the faith.

<small>Bishop Selwyn</small> A few faithful men, by the power of the Spirit of God, have been the instruments of adding another Christian people to the family of God.'

Having acquired the Maori language during the long voyage, Bishop Selwyn found himself on landing capable of addressing the two races over whom he had been placed—races which were being constantly brought into mutual antagonism, to the great hindrance of spiritual work, of whom the weaker has been saved from extinction mainly by the protection which has been given to them by the Church. The bishop at once began to traverse the length and breadth of his diocese, travelling on foot, with some natives carrying his tent, which served the purposes of a church. His first visitation occupied five months, and he returned with his clothes ragged, and his last pair of shoes tied to his insteps by a strip of *Phormium tenax*, avoiding the publicity of the town of Auckland, and making his way over a plot of ground which he had secured for a cathedral of the future, which he hoped 'may hereafter be traversed by the feet of many bishops, better shod and far less ragged than myself.' But he had hardly made himself acquainted with the condition and wants of the diocese before he was confronted with the dissensions and contests of two races, which, with some peaceful intervals, disturbed his whole life in New Zealand. The natives not unnaturally became uneasy as they beheld the rapid increase of the English, who threatened to outnumber themselves. Foreign influences were at work to persuade them that they were the slaves of the English; and the English on their part did not disguise their opinion that the disappearance of the whole Maori race would be welcome to them.

Contests between races

In 1843 there was a great outbreak at the Wairau in the Southern Island arising from a dispute about a sale of land. A party of armed men were led by the English magistrate to enforce his authority; the natives were peaceable and wished to refer the matter to the courts. Without orders, firing began on the part of the English, and the wife of one of the chiefs was killed. Her husband started up and exclaimed, '*Farewell the light! Farewell the day! Come hither night!*' and immediately returned the fire, by which twenty-three persons were killed. In 1844 John Heke, who had been for years living peaceably on a mission station, cut down, after giving due notice of his intention, an obnoxious flagstaff which was supposed to be an emblem of the subjection of his race. He danced a war dance before the bishop; but he warned the civilians of their danger and even helped them to move their belongings. H.M.S. 'Hazard' engaged the natives, and throughout the painful struggle the bishop endeavoured to be the friend of both parties, exercising his office among their wounded indifferently.

Uprisings of the Maoris

From the first Bishop Selwyn determined to rely on the natives for a large share of the work of evangelising their brethren. When the war of races was raging, and some tribes adhered to the English, such work was accompanied with much danger; but the Maori race has very keen spiritual proclivities, and, whatever their failings, cowardice is not among them. In 1846, while the land was much disturbed, the bishop met 2,000 Maoris at Whanganui. They joined in worship and 382 communicated; they then formally determined to send two of their number as evangelists to a tribe with whom they had been at war. They knew the peril, and on their road they were met and warned that they were going to their death. Ten friends accompanied them, and on their way they were fired on by the enemy, who were in ambush. The two teachers were killed, one on the spot, but the other lived long enough to bind up his wounds and to give to the only one of his ten companions who had been injured, his Testament, telling him that that was indeed great riches.

Maori evangelists

Thus the Native Church of New Zealand had its early martyrs. In 1853 the first native deacon, Rota, the equivalent of Lot, as Maoris cannot pronounce 'L,' was ordained. He was the first of nearly forty native clergymen who have been ordained from a race that never at any time exceeded 100,000 in number. Amid all the reverses and fluctuations of the New Zealand Church, even when the Hau-Hau fanaticism took possession of the people, the native clergy have without exception been staunch and faithful.

In 1854 the bishop visited England: there were

many matters which demanded his presence. He returned in 1855 with the Rev. J. C. Patteson, who in 1861 became the first Bishop of Melanesia. The Colonial work of the Church was now developed. The Canterbury settlement brought into the Southern Island a population of a higher class than the ordinary immigrant; and in 1856 the Rev. H. J. C. Harper was consecrated Bishop of Christ Church. In 1858 the dioceses of Nelson and Wellington were founded. There were now four Eton bishops; for Bishop Harper had been a private tutor at Eton, while Bishops Selwyn, Hobhouse, and Abraham had been Eton boys. On this occasion Bishop Selwyn was made Metropolitan, and in the following year Archdeacon Williams was consecrated Bishop of Waiapu. In 1866 the formation of the See of Dunedin gave a sixth bishop to the New Zealand Church, exclusive of the missionary diocese of Melanesia.

Rev. J. C. Patteson

Increase of the New Zealand Episcopate

But in the midst of this progress there burst out in 1862 a serious insurrection, which for long threatened to destroy the whole work of past years. In the Northern Island Wiremu Tamahána, the King-maker as he was called, gathered the Ngatihaua tribe together; the road to Whanganui was closed, and a board was erected demanding a toll of 5*l*. from every settler who should desire to pass, and 50*l*. from every minister of religion, whether native or English. The antipathy to the missionaries arose from the fact that they had openly urged the people to accept what was clearly the will of God and would turn to their advantage, union with the English.

The King-maker and the Land Question

under the common sovereignty of the Queen. The
natives were now persuaded that their teachers had all
along been in the service of the English and had prepared the way for their subjugation. Sir George Grey,
eminent everywhere as the protector of the aborigines
in the various colonies in which he had represented the
Queen, was busy in making roads which should facilitate
peaceful traffic and also the movements of troops in
case of need. The Maoris on their part openly proclaimed their grievances and seized on a block of land
at Tataraimaka as a material guarantee for the restoration of the Waitara, which they declared had never
been ceded. A great gathering was held at the house
of Wiremu Tamahana, which the bishop attended. The
question in dispute was seen to be in itself a small one;
but it represented nothing less than the old question of
nationality. The King-maker himself was moderate in
his counsels. He addressed his followers on a certain
Sunday morning on the words, 'Behold how good and
joyful a thing it is, brethren, to dwell together in unity,'
and he showed the advantages which had accrued from
the union of the Maori tribes under one king. The
bishop, having obtained permission to hold service in
the afternoon, preached a far more comprehensive sermon
on the same text. The next day he gave a remarkable
address to the natives which commenced thus:

'Here am I as mediator for New Zealand. My work
is mediation. I am not merely a Pakeha (Englishman)
or a Maori. I am a half-caste. I have eaten your food.
I have slept in your houses; I have talked with you,
journeyed with you, prayed with you, received the Holy
Communion with you. Therefore I say I am a half-

caste. I cannot rid myself of my half-caste: it is in my body, in my flesh, in my bones, in my sinews. Yes, we are all of us half-caste. Your dress is half-caste, a Maori mat and English clothes; your strength is half-caste, your courage half-caste, the man a Maori, the uniform and word of command, English. Your faith is half-caste, the first preachers, your fathers in God, English; your own hearts the mother in which was born faith. Therefore I say we are all half-castes, therefore let us dwell together with one faith, one land, one love.'

Bishop Selwyn as Mediator

Turning to Wiremu Tamahana, the bishop said, 'My son, here am I, begging you in the name of the dead at Taranaki, agree to these principles.'

Turning to the whole assembly, he said, 'Oh all ye tribes of New Zealand, sitting in council here, I beseech you in the name of our Lord Jesus Christ, in whom we all believe and hope, agree to the proposal by which we shall all live in peace and happiness.'

Some were influenced by the Bishop's words, but further complications arose. The colonists were possessed by fear and hatred of the Maoris. Ten thousand British troops took the field; they had no chaplain, so the Bishop thought his place was with them; but he cared not less for the Maori portion of his common charge, and thus incurred the suspicion of both. He buried the dead in each camp, saying, 'If there must be war, our great effort ought to be to debrutalise it.' In 1864 the war broke out again and the British troops were repulsed with much slaughter; but in time discipline prevailed and the Maoris were defeated. There was no formal termination of the war;

Open war of races

but the Maoris retreated into a territory known as the King's country, which was not acquired by the English for another twenty years. In the midst of this state of war a horrible delusion possessed the minds of a large section of the Maori people. A certain chief had shown such signs of madness that his people had bound him, first with ropes, afterwards with chain and padlock. He made his escape and declared that the angel Gabriel had released him. No longer regarded as insane, he was accepted by the people as a prophet. Soon he was declared to be the angel Gabriel himself. He compiled a form of worship for his followers, which was a mixture of Romanism, Wesleyanism, and Mohammedanism. This creed he determined to propagate by the sword. Under the influence of visions his followers reverted to cannibalism and adopted the Peruvian title of 'Inca' for their priests and leaders. They assumed the Maori equivalent of Catholic, and called their creed 'Pai-Mairire' (all-holy), and themselves Hau-haus, from their habit of barking like dogs. They were conducting their worship in Poverty Bay and uttering a bitter lamentation for the lands which had gone from them, when a little schooner put into the harbour and landed a clergy-

The Hau-hau fanaticism

man, who had long laboured among them, the Rev. C. S. Volkner. The fanatics seized him, dragged him ashore, and intimated that he must die. He refused to believe it, and for a while there seemed to be a wavering among the people. A night of suspense followed. The next morning he busied himself among his people and gave them some little commissions which he had executed for them in Auckland. At 2 P.M. their intentions were made known. They took his clothes from him and led him to a tree. He knelt down and prayed, shook hands with his murderers, and then calmly saying, 'I'm ready,' he was put to death with all the savagery of which infatuated men were capable.

In the midst of these things the Maori clergy were faithful to a man, but the work of years seemed to have come to nought, and the general apostacy of the people seemed at hand. Bishop Selwyn wrote at this time:

<small>Fidelity of Maori clergy</small>

'I have now one simple missionary idea before me, of watching over the remnant that is left. Our work is a remnant in two senses, a remnant of a decaying people and a remnant of a decaying faith. The works of which you hear are not the works of heathens. They are the works of baptized men, whose love has grown cold, from causes common to all churches of neophytes, from Laodicea downwards.'

<small>Declension</small>

The Maoris never recovered wholly from the convulsions in which the faith of many of them was shipwrecked. In the dioceses of Waiapu and Christ Church they have shown great zeal in building their own churches and in forming endowments for their clergy. Meanwhile their numbers are diminishing, and it is computed that, including half-castes, there are not 50,000 remaining. They are all, at least in profession, Christians. In 1868 Bishop Selwyn became Bishop of Lichfield and was succeeded by the Rev. W. G. Cowie, Rector of Stafford, who took the title of Bishop of Auckland.

CHAPTER IX.

MISSIONS IN THE PACIFIC OCEAN.

No mission in modern times, probably no mission in any age of the Church, has attracted more enthusiasm or enlisted more noble workers than the mission to Melanesia. The romance which from the first has accompanied the venture of faith has been of abounding interest. The tragedies which on more than one occasion have marked its career have had a pathos of their own, and the men who planned and have carried out the enterprise have been, one after another, men of chivalrous self-devotion. And yet no attempts have been made to attract especial notice or sympathy. The work has been carried on very quietly, no exaggeration has been indulged in, and even the simple story of the mission has not been widely published nor have importunate appeals for money been put forth.

The Melanesian Mission

It is well known that a clerical error in the letters patent of the first Bishop of New Zealand assigned as the northern limits of his diocese latitude 34° 30′ *north* instead of *south*, a blunder which committed to his charge not less than 68° of latitude more than had been intended. But this error might have been passed over as laying no such burden as a literal acceptance of the document would have entailed. What most weighed with Bishop Selwyn was that on his consecration Archbishop Howley urged him to watch over the interests of religion and the progress of the

Its origin

Gospel in the coasts and islands of the Pacific. In the several groups so widely scattered, Romanists and Nonconformists from Great Britain and from Nova Scotia had commenced work. But the field was absolutely boundless, for the islands were numbered by hundreds. Almost every island had its own language, sometimes more than one; and the number of those which had, ever so slightly, come under a missionary's care, was but a mere fraction of the whole. It is stated on good authority that John Wesley had been so moved by the difficulties of the missionary problem in these regions, that he despaired of the numerous islands being won to the faith. Not only were there the difficulties of a babel of tongues; the climate, especially of the equatorial groups, is ill-suited to English residents; and the people, barbarous and isolated, constantly warring with each other, had no relations with the outer world, even of the elementary kind which gave to Samuel Marsden an entry to New Zealand.

Its difficulties

It was with a full knowledge of all the risks and the probable disappointment that Bishop Selwyn, in 1847, having in five years of work organised his diocese of New Zealand, turned his attention to the Melanesian group. An opportunity of making a tour of inspection under very favourable conditions presented itself. An affray between two British ships and the natives of the island of Rotuma made it necessary that H.M.S. 'Dido' should visit the scene. The 'Dido's' chaplain was ill and was in hospital at Auckland, and the bishop took his place on board. He visited in the Friendly and Navigator groups the stations

Bishop Selwyn's first visit

of the London and Wesleyan Missionary Societies, and he also touched at Anaiteum, the most southern of the New Hebrides group. Where a divided Christendom had made any efforts for the evangelisation of the islands he declined to interfere—the field was so wide, and the unoccupied spaces so large and many. He found the whole of Melanesia open to him. European teacher of any nation or creed there was not; but traders had preceded the evangelist and had dared all the risks.

Nonconformist missions

This was soon impressed upon him at the Isle of Pines, where the people were believed to be exceptionally treacherous. The bishop was advised not to land; but in a little boat he sculled himself round a headland into a lagoon, where he found an English schooner at anchor, and her captain quietly smoking a pipe. He heard from this captain, whom he afterwards called 'my tutor' in recognition of the lesson which he had learned from him, that he had traded with the people of the island for years; that they had cut many thousands of feet of sandal-wood for him and brought it on board the schooner; and that by kindness and fair dealing he had secured a thoroughly friendly understanding with them. That such men as this Captain Paddon should have accomplished so much in the interests of trade, while the Church had done nothing, filled the bishop's soul with compunction, and he wrote to a friend in England in remorseful words:—

Friendly natives of Isle of Pines

'While I have been sleeping in my bed in New Zealand, these islands, the Isle of Pines, New Caledonia, New Hebrides, New Ireland, New Britain, New Guinea, the Loyalty Islands, the Kingsmills, &c., &c.,

have been riddled through and through by the whale-fishers and traders of the South Sea. That odious black slug, the bêche-de-mer, has been dragged out of its hole in every coral reef, to make black broth for Chinese mandarins, by the unconquerable daring of English traders, while I, like a worse black slug as I am, have left the world all its field of mischief to itself. The same daring men have robbed every one of these islands of its sandal-wood, to furnish incense for the idolatrous worship of the Chinese temples, before I have taught a single islander to offer up his sacrifice of prayer to the true and only God. Even a mere Sydney speculator could induce nearly a hundred men from some of the wildest islands in the Pacific to sail in his ships to Sydney to keep his flocks and herds, before I, to whom the Chief Shepherd has given commandment to seek out His sheep that are scattered over a thousand isles, have sought out or found so much as one of those which have strayed and are lost.'

The bishop saw enough on his first visit to convince him that the ordinary method of placing European teachers on the islands, even could he have obtained them in sufficient numbers, was altogether incompatible with the conditions under which the evangelisation of these remote islands could be accomplished. Indepen-

Babel of tongues dently of the question of health, on which there could be little doubt, the babel of languages was a problem of extreme difficulty, with which he became personally impressed, for he wrote:—

'Nothing but a special interposition of the Divine power could have produced such a babel of tongues as we find here. In islands not larger than the Isle of

Wight, we find dialects so distinct that the inhabitants of the various districts hold no communication with each other. Here have I been for a fortnight working away, as I supposed, at the language of New Caledonia, and just when I have begun to see my way, and to be able to communicate a little with an Isle of Pines boy, whom I found here, I learn that this is only a dialect used in the southern extremity of the island, and not understood in the part which I wish to attack first.'

Therefore the bishop saw that from the multitude of islands, each with its own tongue, individuals must be brought for instruction to one common centre, and taught in one common language, and be thence sent back each to their own homes and races, to impart what they had learned. In New Zealand there appeared to be such a centre; but the difficulty now immediate was how to obtain such representatives. This was a work which might have daunted the bravest spirit; but in 1849 Bishop Selwyn made the attempt, and started, not without much anxiety on the part of his friends, in a little vessel of twenty tons, the 'Undine.' Every additional ton added to the cost of sails, cordage, and hands. The bishop was most scrupulous in reducing the expenditure of mission money; and in this little yacht, with the good hand of God upon him, he sailed, from first to last, more than twenty thousand miles without the loss of a spar. Amid the islands he fell in with H.M.S. 'Havannah,' and impressed the captain and crew with the highest respect for his intrepidity. He allowed no arms to be carried on board his yacht, and his method of opening communications with the people was both original and bold. Pulling

Mission formally commenced

towards the beach, he would wade or swim through the surf, leaving the boat outside as a precaution. No women would appear; but the natives, armed with spears or poisoned arrows, would stand on the coral beach to receive the strange visitor. By manner and gesture the bishop would show that he came with peace; a few presents would be given, a few names of chiefs or of lads written down, a few words of their language learned and noted, and the visit would be at an end. Nothing would have been done, so far as outward seeming was concerned; but, for those who could patiently wait, much had been done. Confidence had been gained; a good feeling established; the visit was an event which would be remembered, differing as it did from the visits of traders or of sailors, who put in to get fresh water; and when he came again, the bishop would not come as a stranger; the women would then appear, and possibly a boy or two would be entrusted to the bishop's care. In this visit of 1849, the bishop succeeded beyond his expectation. From the three islands of Lifu, Maré, and New Caledonia he brought away five boys, whose friends allowed him to take them to New Zealand. This was a good beginning, and he reached his own house at Auckland in the early hours of the morning, exclaiming to the just awakened household, 'I'VE GOT THEM.' These lads were the forerunners of the native Melanesian ministry, the almost unconscious grammars and dictionaries by which the white man was about to conquer the difficulties of their manifold tongues.

<small>First pupils brought to New Zealand</small>

'*In I am, and on I must,*' the bishop declared to be now his monosyllabic motto. He saw how vast was the opening for work, and he recognised the wisdom of securing for it more support and co-operation. In 1850 he went to Sydney, where he met in council the five Australian bishops, and among other results of the conference was the establishment of an Australasian Board of Missions, whereby the Melanesian Mission was formally adopted by those dioceses as the scene of their evangelistic work. Not merely sympathy and money were promised, but it was agreed that the bishops of Australia would take their share in the conduct of the mission. Much enthusiasm was stirred up, and the Churchmen of New South Wales gave to the work a larger vessel than the 'Undine,' the 'Border Maid.' In this schooner the Bishop of Newcastle accompanied the Bishop of New Zealand in 1852, but this was the solitary instance in which personal assistance was given by Australia. The cruise was a remarkable one, and not without much risk. At one of the New Hebrides Islands a plan had been formed to cut off the ship and to seize the bishop; but adverse winds prevented him approaching the island. At Malicolo, in the same group, Bishop Selwyn had gone ashore with the boats for water, leaving on board the Bishop of Newcastle, the mate, and two or three sailors. Many canoes surrounded the ship, and the natives, with no attempt to conceal their intentions, endeavoured to board her, but were overawed by the presence and manner of Bishop Tyrrell, who had no arms on board. At last, after conference, the canoes made for the shore, where hundreds of armed men were standing brandishing their clubs and threatening the men who were left in charge of the boats. It was a

The Council of Australasian Bishops, 1850

moment of great anxiety. The little company on board prayed earnestly for the deliverance of their friends; and on the shore Bishop Selwyn, detecting the evil purpose of the people, retreated to the boats, and made his escape under a shower of arrows. The cruise extended to the Solomon Islands, and thirteen new scholars were brought to New Zealand.

In 1854 Bishop Selwyn visited England and provided for the division of his diocese which was accomplished in 1856 and the two following years. He returned in 1855 with the Rev. J. C. Patteson as his chaplain, and was followed by a new mission ship, the 'Southern Cross.'

Rev. J. C. Patteson and the 'Southern Cross'

On Mr. Patteson the chief burden of the Melanesian work henceforth devolved. At this time several important changes occurred in the islands themselves. France took possession of New Caledonia and the Loyalty Group, in which the London Missionary Society had long had stations; at Norfolk Island the descendants of the mutineers of the 'Bounty' had been settled by Government, deserting their former home on Pitcairn's Island. It had become clear to Bishop Selwyn that Auckland was too cold in the winter for the residence of the island pupils, and that, to avoid the interruption of their education caused by their return to their homes during the comparatively cold months and the cost of such frequent voyages, a permanent settlement must be made in some island not too hot for Europeans nor too cold for the lads. In Norfolk Island it seemed that the right place was found; but difficulties arose, and at great cost a college was built at Kohimārama, near Auckland, where the work was carried on for some years under many disadvantages. Mr. Patteson spent one winter with his pupils on the Island of Lifu, and another at Mota; but these were dangerous and unsatisfactory experiments, and in 1867 the mission was finally established on Norfolk Island as its head-quarters.

This, however, is in anticipation of the story. Before he went to England, Bishop Selwyn had visited more than fifty islands, and had received, in all, forty pupils speaking ten distinct languages. In 1857, with a new ship and a colleague in Mr. Patteson, who had already entered into the spirit of the work, a very memorable voyage was made, in which sixty islands were touched, some of them nearer to the equator than any which the Bishop had reached before, and thirty-three new scholars were brought to New Zealand. This period *Progress of the mission* was altogether a remarkable one in the history of the Missions. The people of Anaiteum had in nine years become Christians, to the number of 4,000; two chapels and nearly fifty schoolrooms had been built, and heathenism was at an end. This was the work of *Success of the Nonconformist missionaries* Nonconformists, who seemed to have made provision for occupying the southern portion of Melanesia. The northern islands, far less healthy and more remote, seemed at the same time to present themselves and to offer their children freely. The Banks' Islands afforded a safe harbourage and a convenient water station. At Mai, in the centre of the New Hebrides, was found a people whose language was akin to Maori, and these sent a chief as a scholar. So year by year the work went on. School work and domestic work produced the results of wholesome discipline. The communal life of teachers and pupils avoided all questions of masters and servants; everything had to be done by the teachers in the first place, and the imitative powers of the pupils made them efficient helpers. By the direct teaching of their countrymen, as they returned to their homes, the barbarous habits of the people were subdued and changed, and civilisation and religion were spreading in many directions through unconscious instruments. Sickness now and again turned the school into a hospital and the teachers into nurses; but the relations of the two were made closer and more affectionate by the trouble. At length the prophecy of Bishop Selwyn, when he wrote in his diary in 1852, 'The careful superintendence of this multitude of islands will require the services of a missionary bishop able and willing to devote himself to this work,' reached its accomplishment. On St. Matthias' Day, 1861, the Rev. J. C. Patteson was consecrated Bishop of Melanesia, and took absolute charge of the whole work. It is needless to follow the history of the mission year by year, when each year did but reproduce with accidental variation the events of the preceding. In 1864 the mission ship was attacked by the natives of Santa Cruz, and two young men from Norfolk Island, Edwin Nobbs and Fisher Young, died of their wounds. In 1868 George Sarawia, who, until Bishop Selwyn landed on his island in 1858 had never seen a white man, was ordained deacon, the first member of the many tribes of Melanesia to be admitted into the ministry.

Consecration of Bishop Patteson

But while this work of love and mercy was being extended, other works of a far different kind were spreading and were destined in time to arrest the labours of Bishop Patteson and his colleagues. The planters in Queensland wanted cheap labour. There was no properly organised system of coolie labour, and an abominable trade had sprung up among the islands which was nothing short of man-stealing. Pirate ships approached the islands, sometimes with professions of a desire to trade, and it is recorded that the 'Southern Cross' and the bishop himself were personated in order to deceive the people. The islanders were brought on board, sometimes by fraud, sometimes by force, and then the ship would sail away with its captives in the very presence of the canoes of their friends, and the poor slaves were deported to Australia. This led to many reprisals, of which Bishop Patteson was quite aware. The contact of these traders aroused the worst suspicions and passions of the untaught man, and the bishop protested against any revenge being executed should he himself fall a victim. In 1871 five men had been forcibly carried away from Nukapu, and the people determined to revenge themselves on the first white men who came within their reach. In September 1871, Bishop Patteson landed on the little island. There were seen four canoes hovering to windward and not approaching the schooner as usual; so the boat was lowered and the bishop pulled towards the shore. The tide was low and the boat could not cross the reef, so he got into a canoe manned by two chiefs whom he knew, and was taken ashore. In a short time a flight of poisoned arrows was directed at the boat, and the Rev. J. Atkin and two natives were mortally wounded. The boat went back to the ship, and,

The labour vessels

returning with a rising tide, pulled into the lagoon, her party having grave forebodings as to the fate of the bishop. There they found the murdered body laid, not without care and reverence, in a canoe which was drifting towards the ship. A native mat tied round the neck and ankles covered the body, and into the folds of the breast a palm branch was thrust, with five knots tied in it. The old law of retaliation had prompted the deed, and the five knots showed that the five friends, who had been carried into captivity fraudulently were avenged. It was a time in which the mission was tried to the uttermost; the scholars proved themselves equal to the occasion, and relieved the English teachers of many things which they had previously done. The Rev. R. H. Codrington visited Queensland in the hope of recovering the men who had been kidnapped. In Australia and in England the noble life and death of Bishop Patteson was received with an emotion that is rarely witnessed. The Queen's speech at the opening of Parliament in 1872 alluded to the tragic end of so noble a life. The Propagation Society raised to the memory of the martyred bishop a large sum of money which has been devoted to the endowment of the See, to the erection of a church at Norfolk Island which personal friends have freely adorned, and to the purchase of a new ship. Bishop Selwyn, who was then Bishop of Lichfield, stated at Oxford that at the time of his death 'Bishop Patteson had 565 young islanders under his care, that he had established so great a confidence among the islanders that it was only a question of how many the 'Southern Cross' could bring back on her voyages, and that there were 160 scholars, speaking not less than fifteen languages, under instruction at Norfolk Island.'

In February 1873 the Rev. J. R. Selwyn and J. Still joined Mr. Codrington, the head of the mission, and the work went on in all directions as though no such calamity as that of Nukapu had befallen it. In 1875 the 'Southern Cross' conveyed Mr. Selwyn to Sydney, where Bishop Barker had the privilege of confirming twelve Melanesian candidates. With an increased staff the members now dispersed themselves, several making up their minds to spend a solitary three or four months' visit on one of the islands without any European companion; such visits have won confidence, have dispelled fears, and have advanced greatly the whole work of the mission.

<small>Rev. J. R. Selwyn and J. Still join the mission</small>

At length, in February 1877, after an interregnum of more than five years, the Rev. J. R. Selwyn was consecrated at Nelson the successor to Bishop Patteson, a solemn service of intercession being held at the same hour (11 P.M.) in Lichfield Cathedral. The thoughts suggested both contrast and unity. While the Lichfield congregation came through the cold and darkness of a winter's night into the brightly lighted cathedral, into the simple church at Nelson, 8,000 miles in a direct line beneath our feet, the floods of noonday sun were shining, and all around the ripened corn was waving in the fresh sea-breeze; but the prayers that came from hearts separated by half the globe met before the Throne. In 1879 the beautiful memorial church at Norfolk Island began to be used, but it was not consecrated until December 1880, when,

<small>Mr. Selwyn consecrated bishop</small>

in the presence of the Bishop of Auckland and visitors from England as well as from New Zealand, the church was solemnly dedicated to the worship of God.

It was now felt to be a main duty of the mission to recover the confidence of the people at Nukapu and at Santa Cruz, where, as has been mentioned, two members had been killed in 1864. The difficulty had not become less by time, for H.M.S. 'Rosario' was sent, in defiance of the protest uttered by Bishop Patteson long before, to avenge his death. An action had been fought in which the islanders had shown great courage; but the guns of a man-of-war destroyed at long range the villages and the homes and slaughtered the people whom the bishop had loved so well. Then in 1875 another encounter had taken place at Santa Cruz, in which Commodore Goodenough, a most humane and gallant officer, had been killed. In 1877 the 'Southern Cross' had visited Nukapu and learned from eye-witnesses some particulars of the bishop's death, but no permanent stay was effected. In the following year, by his own desire, a native deacon, Wadrokal, took possession of the Reef Islands near to Santa Cruz, from which it was hoped that Santa Cruz itself might be reached. In 1880 the 'Southern Cross' visited him and found with him some natives of Santa Cruz, to whom the bishop proposed that they should go with him to their home and introduce him to their people; they jumped at the idea, and almost without difficulty the landing was effected, and Wadrokal and his wife were left to dwell among the people, with the consent of all. Returning a few weeks later the bishop found them comfortably settled and the people attentive

Confidence of natives recovered

and willing. Thus Santa Cruz was regained. Nukapu was felt to be easier to win, and in 1884 the bishop went there carrying on board the ship a lofty memorial cross, which the Patteson family had desired to have erected near the scene of their relative's murder, at a spot whence it would look across the waters of the Pacific and tell the story of peace and love and reconciliation. The people were consulted, and they asked with superstitious fear whether it was intended to work harm to them; on being told of the loving tidings of which it was a silent witness they assisted in its erection, and of their own accord, before the bishop sailed away, they had begun to cut down trees and to build a fence round it.

The bishop visited England in 1885, and could state that the last year had been the brightest and most hopeful of his episcopate; progress was to be discerned everywhere and special blessings had filled the hearts of the missionaries with thankfulness. The labour trade Present condition of the mission has now come under very stringent regulations of the Queensland Government, and the High Commissioner has forbidden the sale of firearms throughout the South Pacific. Printing-presses are at work in each group of islands, giving to each the word of life in its own tongue, and at Norfolk Island 170 students are being trained to carry back to their island homes the lessons of holy living and holy teaching which they have themselves received.

In the Southern Pacific lies the youngest of English colonies, the Fiji Islands, whose people are the transition-link between the black and copper-coloured races of Polynesia and Melanesia. Ecclesiastically Fiji is a waif, attached neither to the Australian nor to the New Zealand Church, and the Archipelago lies too far away from Norfolk Island to allow of its forming a part of the charge of Bishop Selwyn. Of the 250 islands of which the group consists, 80 are inhabited. Long before the cession of the islands to Great Britain in 1874 Romanists and Wesleyans had laboured for their conversion, and the latter body has carried on a work of unusual magnitude and success. Nominally at least the whole of the native population is Christian, the majority being Wesleyans. The white colonists at present number about 3,000, of whom the greater number reside at Suva and Levuka, but there are small colonies on other islands. Coolie labourers have been introduced from the Melanesian Islands and from North India, about 7,000 from the former, and 4,000 from the latter.

<small>Fiji</small>

<small>Early and successful missions</small>

The first Governor, the Hon. Sir Arthur H. Gordon, has been eminent, in the several governments which he has administered, for his scrupulous regard for the rights of the people of the country. He was appointed also High Commissioner for the Western Pacific, and continued, after his resignation of the governorship, by orders of H. M. Government at home, to be consulted on certain branches of the administration of Fiji. At Sir A. Gordon's invitation, Bishop Selwyn visited the islands in 1880, not as having any authority, but because many of his own people were settled there and no other bishop was likely to undertake the charge of the colony, which by a legal fiction is attached to the diocese of London. In a stay of three weeks he admitted a catechist to deacon's orders, confirmed many

<small>Hon. Sir A. H. Gordon</small>

persons, and held services on several islands. He was much impressed by the thoroughness of the work of the Wesleyan missionaries; but in view of the increasing numbers of the colonists, and of coolies, and of his own inability to undertake the charge, he was convinced of the necessity of the islands having a bishop resident on the spot. A munificent Australian settler, already known as the founder of one and the part founder of two bishoprics, *Proposed bishopric of Fiji* announced his intention of devoting the proceeds of the sale of an estate in Fiji to the endowment of the see. But land, there as elsewhere, is at the present time depreciated in value, and the generous intention has had to be postponed.

In the Northern Pacific another group of islands forms an outpost of the English Church. Eight islands, 'resting like a bunch of water-lilies on the bosom of the ocean,' were discovered by Captain Cook in 1778. The natives called the largest one Hawaii; but Cook named the whole group after his patron, the Earl of Sandwich. *Hawaiian Islands* The surroundings of the famous sailor, his ships, so vast in comparison with the largest of their canoes, his guns and the effect produced by firing them, his clothes and those of his sailors, impressed the islanders with the belief that their new visitor was more than mortal; and there is reason to believe that he favoured the superstition and accepted not merely homage and consideration but even worship from them. But in time the people lost their illusions; disputes arose, and Captain Cook was killed at Kealakeakua Bay. Vancouver, who had been a companion of Cook, visited the islands about 1792. He gave the people sheep, and cattle, and some seeds. Knowing something of their language, he spoke to them of sacred things; and on his departure he carried with him to England a request for Christian teachers, which was actually delivered to Mr. Pitt, but no teachers were sent. The people were to get the elements of Christianity from other and strange sources. Whalers visited the harbours of Hawaii from time to time; their intercourse with the people was not of an elevating kind; disputes and fights and murders frequently happened. In 1786 the king seized on two English sailors named Young and Davis in revenge for a murder perpetrated by others. They were not punished, but were treated with kindness, and by their superior civilisation they rose to be chiefs. The king and his people were living under the burden of the native superstitions, of which the Tapu (taboo), already mentioned, was the most grievous. The white men, it was observed, paid no heed to it, and yet lived without any open judgment on their impiety. The king would enjoy equal liberty if he dared. He had heard too that some of the Southern Islands far away had thrown away the bondage which held him fast and had embraced the white man's religion. From the two sailors he sought for such instruction as they were able *Idolatry abandoned* to give, and when he died, in 1819, he had abjured heathenism, while he had had no opportunity of being built up in Christianity. His son and successor determined to break up the system under which his people groaned. He gave a state banquet, at which it was a matter of religious obligation that the men should sit at one table and the women by themselves at another. Ostentatiously he took his seat with the Queen Dowager. The people looked, expecting a visible token of vengeance; but when no harm befell they declared the 'tapu' to be at an end, and throughout the islands a general and simultaneous destruction of idols took place, in which the priests joined. Not fewer than 40,000 idols were destroyed in a few days, although up to this time no Christian teaching, other than that which the English sailors had given, had ever reached the islands. In 1820 America sent some Congregationalists; but the people were still awaiting the English teachers for whom they had asked, and there was some hesitation about allowing the mission to be established. In 1822 the London Missionary Society sent some teachers, who acquired the language and made grammars and dictionaries. In 1823 the King Kamehameha II. and his queen visited England, and stated to George IV. in pathetic terms that their former idolatrous system had been abolished and that they wished the English Protestant religion to be practised in Hawaii. What might have been the result of their prayer, had they lived, cannot be surmised. The king and queen, weakened by a long and trying voyage, succumbed to the rigours of a London winter, and another king, Kamehameha III., reigned until 1855. In 1829 the Roman Church sent some priests to Hawaii; but the Congregationalists had obtained much political influence, and they prevented their settlement, until in 1839 a French frigate enforced the religious toleration which the Nonconformists had refused.

With the accession in 1855 of Kamehameha IV. a new era was opened for the islands. He was a man of great natural powers, and had had the advantage of travelling in England, France, and the

Kamehameha IV.

United States. He had married the grand-daughter of John Young, the English sailor, an educated and devout woman, well known up to the time of her death in 1884 as Queen Emma. The king was a student of theology and much attached to the English Church, whose Prayer Book he had translated for the benefit of his subjects, and he had added an original preface in which he set forth his own belief, and his reasons for preferring the Anglican Church to the other denominations which were known to his people. In 1860 he repeated the request for English teachers made by his ancestor seventy years before, and in 1861 a bishop and three clergymen were sent out. The king and queen were confirmed: together they became sponsors for numbers of children for whose religious education they pledged themselves: schools were built, stations were opened on other islands, and a system of religious education was established throughout the little kingdom. But all this fair promise received a check when, in 1863, the king died. The mission has had ever since to rely on its inherent strength rather than on royal favour. Nor can it be said to have failed under the trial. It has had many disappointments: the loss of the king, the early withdrawal of the bishop and first missionary party, the failure of the early supporters in England to continue the pecuniary help which they had promised, the burden of a costly cathedral, the mere foundations of which cost much money that had been more wisely spent in living agency. Then in the work itself there have been special difficulties. The white population have not cared to support the mission. Political matters, alto-

The English mission founded

Disappointments

gether irrevelant, have needlessly been introduced, to the increase of prejudice; and the natives, themselves rapidly passing away, the victims of their own vices and of those of their forefathers, do not satisfy the expectations of those, if such there be, who can work only under the hope and expectation of speedy and visible results. Nevertheless the patience of Bishop Willis has had its fruits, now visible to all men. He has cared for the remnant of the race without thought of how long they will last. His communities of sisters have shown themselves to be well adapted for the work, requiring so much mingled gentleness and firmness, of educating the young and restoring the fallen members of a race with such a history as the Hawaiians have. His cathedral, more modest in its actual existence than in the visions of the early promoters of the scheme, is rapidly rising, suitable stone having been found within easy distance. His eight clergy, with an equal number of laymen, meet in synod. Finally, the work among the Chinese coolies on the sugar estates has been very successful, the people subscribing willingly and liberally to the support of their teachers and to the cost of building two churches.

<small>Progress</small>

The late Bishop Wilberforce, who was much interested in the Hawaiian Church, was wont to express a hope that the Bishop of Melanesia might go northwards and the Bishop of Honolulu southwards on their several errands of mercy until the two bishops met on some jointly conquered island, and recognised what God had permitted them to do. The pious hope has not yet been accomplished; but the Hawaiian Church, feeling the evil of isolation, has made proposals to the Church of

New Zealand that it should be admitted into the ecclesiastical province and become part of its provincial system. There can be no doubt of the wisdom of the proposal. Either in union with New Zealand or with the Missionary Churches of Japan, the outpost in the Hawaiian Islands has doubtless before it a work to do, filling up the barren spaces, and linking together the widely-severed Churches of our Communion.

CHAPTER X.

THE CHURCH IN SOUTH AFRICA.

THE Cape Colony, although a British possession, is very largely a Dutch settlement. Holland possessed it for more than a hundred and fifty years before it passed into the hands of Great Britain in 1806. The Dutch East India Company had found it a valuable resting-place on the route to India. In 1795 it had lapsed to France, and was seized by England, but surrendered to the Dutch by the treaty of Amiens. In 1806, war having again broken out, it was taken, after a fierce resistance, by the British. Among those present at the Battle of Blaauwberg was Henry Martyn, who was on his voyage to India. He ministered to the wounded and dying on the field, and prayed 'that the capture of the Cape might be ordered to the advancement of Christ's kingdom, and that England might show herself great indeed by sending forth the ministers of her Church to diffuse the Gospel of peace.' The Dutch had found the Hottentots in possession of the land.

[marginal note: Early settlement in South Africa.]

They are believed to be the aborigines of the country, and are allied to the Copts. They are now, however, almost extinct, the Griquas, a race of mixed blood, being their descendants. Another large nation, with many tribes, supposed to be of Arab origin, were the Kafirs (Infidels), so-called by the Mohammedan nations on the

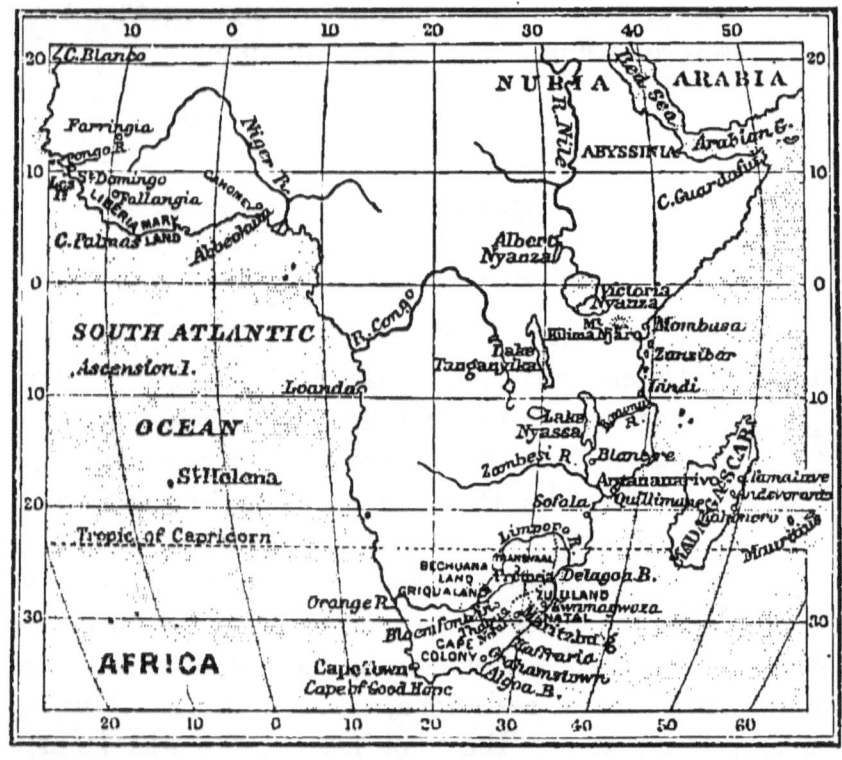

West coast, as they came in contact with them on their way to the South.

The Dutch made very slight religious impression on the country. They forbad the excellent Moravians to minister to the Hottentots, whom they had enslaved, and even where, in rare instances, masters taught their slaves some Christian truths, they

The Dutch

would not allow them to be baptized, because by the law of the country baptism would have set them free of their servitude. England followed only too closely the example of Holland. It extended to the Moravian Brethren the countenance and protection which the Dutch had refused to them. It sent out in 1806 a colonial chaplain for British subjects, and it maintained and even extended the Dutch establishment; but neither for the large number of troops nor for the increasing tide of immigrants was any provision made. Such chaplains as there were in the colony were subject to the control only of the Governor, who was styled 'ex officio ordinary,' even so recently as 1854, although a bishop was appointed in 1847. The Governor licensed the clergy, issued marriage licences, and in him such churches as were built were vested. The Propagation Society sent out a clergyman in 1820, and others followed him at infrequent intervals. In 1827, the third Bishop of Calcutta (James), on leaving England, was authorised by a special commission from the Crown to commence his episcopal functions at the Cape; and the Government Gazette published at Capetown an official notice of the bishop's intended visit 'for the purpose of conferring confirmation upon the British youth of the colony.' Bishop James's episcopate was very brief; and in 1829 his successor, Bishop Turner, landed in Simon's Bay, and spent ten days on shore. In 1832 Bishop Daniel Wilson spent some days at Capetown, and held the first ordination of the English Church in Africa, under a commission from the Bishop of London. In 1843 Bishop Nixon, the

The English

Inadequate spiritual provision

Visits of bishops on their voyage to India and Australia

first Bishop of Tasmania, arrived at Table Bay. He held several Confirmation services, at which 'many hundreds were confirmed,' no opportunity having presented itself since 1832, and he consecrated a church at Simonstown. In 1847 Bishop Gray was consecrated Bishop of Capetown, his jurisdiction extending over 'the whole Colony of the Cape, with its dependencies, and St. Helena.' This included the Cape Colony, Natal, British Kaffraria, the sovereignty now known as the Orange Free State, and St. Helena, in addition to Ascension and Tristan d'Acunha. He found eleven churches, thirteen clergymen, and one catechist. In 1820 the Government voted 50,000*l.* to promote emigration to the Cape, and 4,000 persons availed themselves of the opportunity. In 1836 the Dutch, disliking British rule, travelled, with their cattle and belongings, northward and eastward, and laid the foundation of a colony in Natal, in the Orange Free State, and in the Transvaal. The room which they thus left vacant was instantly filled up by immigrants from England, of whom it was believed 50,000 arrived in one year.

First Bishop of Capetown

The Kafirs, who had waged war with our troops in 1834, were now harassing the Government by the second Kafir war; and the famous chiefs Sandilli, Umhala, and Kreli, afterwards known in connection with the missions of the Church, gave the gallant Sir Harry Smith a high opinion of their courage and their strategic skill. In 1848 the bishop made a tour of 3,000 miles, lasting four months, welcomed everywhere by Moravians, Independents, Presbyterians, and Wesleyans. In 1850, he started on Easter

The Kafirs

Monday, and returned home on Christmas Eve, having spent nine months in incessant travel, sleeping on the ground, or in his waggon, when not near to one of the widely-scattered towns. He had seen Kreli and the other chiefs, and had obtained from them promises of land and of protection; but on the day on which he completed his long journey, the last Kafir war broke out, and all plans for the Eastern Province, where under Bishops Armstrong, Cotterill, and Merriman missions have developed with exceptional success, had to be given up. In 1849 the bishop reached St. Helena, confirmed 500 persons, and consecrated a church at Jamestown. In 1853 Bishop Gray, having thoroughly grasped the needs of the whole region committed to him, and having also quadrupled the number of clergy and seen many churches begun, if not in all cases completed, returned to England and obtained a division of his diocese, the Rev. J. Armstrong and the Rev. J. W. Colenso being consecrated Bishops of Grahamstown and Natal respectively.

Division of the diocese

The Bishop of Capetown was now constituted metropolitan; but an error on the part of the law officers of the Crown led to much litigation at a later time, when it was decided that the Crown had no power to confer a jurisdiction which in terms it had professed to confer. These pages will not enter into the long and painful controversies which both at home and in the Cape Colony characterised the episcopate of Bishop Gray and have much hindered spiritual growth. They are concerned rather with the chronicle of such spiritual growth, which has been, in spite of unusual obstacles, hardly equalled in any other

Litigation

part of the world. With a reduced diocese Bishop Gray's master mind looked out far beyond its limits; not, indeed, to the neglect of his proper work, for his constant journeyings, his lavish liberality, his influence which prompted the colonists to do their share in building up the Church, his careful organisation of synodal action, his employment of the services of faithful women, all these gave to his diocese a prominence which was unrivalled. In 1859 he saw St. Helena made into a separate diocese; in 1861 he consecrated the first bishop of Central Africa; in 1863 he obtained a bishop for the Orange Free State; and when in 1872 he sank under the burdens of an arduous life, he left a province of seven dioceses instead of the one which he had been called to fill, 132 clergymen instead of thirteen, churches built, congregations well established and foundations laid on which those who should come after him would build the more easily. This his successor, Bishop Jones, has found. In spite of many controversies, into which these pages do not enter, the church in South Africa has continued to make spiritual progress, and, even in a time of great commercial disturbance and anxiety, has, by the devotion of its members, been well sustained in material things.

When Bishop Armstrong went out in 1854 he had the whole of the eastern province and British Kaffraria for his episcopal charge. There was also Independent Kaffraria, now the diocese of St. John's, which presented many openings. To quote his own words, he determined that the Church should 'break bounds' and enter on this region also. The time was opportune; the country was weary of costly wars, and

Grahamstown

was willing to spend money on more worthy objects. The Governor, Sir George Grey, already known for his wisdom in dealing with the Maoris, was willing to spend 45,000*l*. per annum for the elevation of the Kafirs. The Propagation Society made itself responsible for large expenditure in view of the exceptional opportunity. The land had been prepared for the seed, for Archdeacon Merriman had gone on foot from one end to the other of the diocese and had made himself known to all races. Umhala, Sandilli, and Kreli, the three chiefs whom Bishop Gray had seen on his first journey, now gladly received the missionaries, and another mission to Kafirs was opened in Grahamstown itself. Bishop Armstrong was followed in 1856 by Bishop Cotterill, whose long episcopate witnessed great extensions of missionary work and missionary success—not, indeed, without some serious disappointments. Hardly had Bishop Armstrong died when a terrible delusion swept over the land. A Kafir, living near the mouth of the Kei River, related the dreams of a girl who professed to have heard the voices of departed chiefs commanding the whole people to slaughter their cattle, a promise being given that if this were done the ancestors of the race and all their cattle would come to life again and the cornpits be filled with corn. The dire command was obeyed; corn and millet were thrown away; cattle were everywhere slaughtered; and as January 11, 1857, the time foretold for the resurrection of the chiefs of the race and their cattle, drew near, the whole people were on the verge of starvation. Many were found dead, their famine-belts drawn tight round their

<small>Kafir delusion.</small>

emaciated bodies; some came to the English in the towns and were thankful to take service, and a large number of children were received at the mission stations. With these terrible sufferings the delusion passed away, and the people, free from their infatuation, recognised the kindness of the missionaries and were more inclined to listen to them. More missions were established, and the Propagation Society maintained a long chain of Kafir stations extending from the city of Grahamstown to Griqualand. In 1860 H.R.H. Prince Alfred visited St. Mark's, where in 1855 the Rev. H. T. Waters had established himself, with wife and children, in a little hut on the banks of the White Kei River, in the midst of the Kafir nation, with no white man near him. At this spot he remained, with no wistful looks towards England, until his death in 1883, his service in Africa having commenced so long ago as 1848. Only three years had elapsed since the delusion, already mentioned, had stalked like a pestilence through the land, when the Amatoza tribe presented an address to Prince Alfred, expressing their gratitude for Sir G. Grey's kind policy 'after we had blindly followed the words of our false prophet and had killed our cattle and destroyed our corn,' and for the fact that 'forty of our sons are learning useful trades in the mission schools.' At his death Archdeacon Waters left St. Mark's a flourishing village, with church, parsonage, schoolhouses, stores and workshops, filled with an industrious and prosperous community, mainly Christian, with a resident magistrate and all the appliances of civilisation around them. The solitary clergyman, who, in 1855, occupied in the name of the Church the vast territory,

Progress

had now become one of twenty under a resident bishop. Other religious bodies had also entered the land where Mr. Waters had been a pioneer; and to the Wesleyans, the Presbyterians, and the Congregationalists is due a share of the glory which belongs to those who have contributed to the changed aspect of the land. The 'rain-doctor' who had lived in comfort in a pastoral land where rain, in frequent and copious supply, is a condition of prosperity, found his occupation gone; and instead of paying fees to this tyrannical impostor the people were wont to request the clergy to pray for rain and to set apart a day of thanksgiving for the ingathering of the harvest.

In 1871 the election of Bishop Cotterill to the See of Edinburgh was followed by the election of Dean Merriman, who had for so many years been Archdeacon of Grahamstown, as his successor. The new Bishop of Edinburgh urged the Scottish Church to undertake the support of a bishop in Kaffraria. To this office the Rev. Dr. Callaway, who had been labouring among the Kafirs in Natal for nearly twenty years, was consecrated in Edinburgh in 1873. For the work of an evangelist he had abandoned a lucrative practice as a medical man in London, and, without any break, had so laboured among the people as to have acquired an intimate knowledge of their modes of thought, their folk-lore, and their language. His manifold gifts, as physician, farmer, printer, as well as priest, had been freely exercised for their benefit, and he was now recognised by the people as indeed their father in God. He had already presented for ordination two natives, whose blameless career had testified

Kaffraria

to the wisdom and power of their teacher. He now determined to establish himself and a group of institutions on the banks of the St. John's River at Umtata. In 1877 the Kafir outbreak occurred, which for some years involved the country in war and made it necessary to proclaim in certain districts martial law. This almost confined the clergy to work in the immediate neighbourhood of their stations; in some cases they had to fly for their lives. But their labours at translating English works into the vernacular were continued, and it is a gratifying fact that not a single Kafir who had been trained in any of the diocesan institutions was disloyal, while many bore arms in the native levies and not a few died fighting for the Queen. In 1879 Bishop Callaway laid the foundation-stone of his training college. In the midst of the ceremony, while the few English settlers were one by one laying their offerings on the stone, Gangalizwe, a famous warrior chief of the Tembu tribe, rode up with a regiment of his cavalry. Dismounting he reverently offered 10*l.*; chief after chief followed his example, and many of the natives gave offerings of sheep and cattle. But the next year the clouds descended again and the war was fiercer than ever. A native catechist was killed at All Saints' Mission, and several stations which had been centres of light were desolated and destroyed.

<small>Loyalty of Kafir Converts</small>

In 1882 Bishop Merriman, who for thirty-three years had been incessantly travelling over an unsettled country without personal injury, was thrown from a pony carriage almost at his own door. He lived for a few days, 'the whole burthen of his delirium being *pro ecclesiâ Dei*—the clergy who wanted help, the

<small>Bishop Merriman</small>

schools, the native clergy, the missions, all passing in rapid succession through his fevered brain.' There have been few greater missionaries than he; regardless of self, avoiding publicity, he went on his way, never turning to look back. He found six clergymen in his archdeaconry in 1848, he left it two dioceses with seventy-two clergymen, of whom nine were natives of the land. He was succeeded by the Bishop of Bloemfontein.

In 1883 the age and weakness of Bishop Callaway made it necessary that he should have a coadjutor in the work of his diocese, and on August 12 the Rev. Bransby Key, an alumnus of St. Augustine's College, Canterbury, was consecrated with the right of succession. He had been the founder of St. Augustine's mission on the borders of Natal, and had laboured there for sixteen years and had suffered probably more than any of his brethren from the troubles and disturbances of the land; but he had won the respect of the natives, and his election was unanimous on the part of both the laity and the clergy of the synod.

Bishop Key

The colony of Natal has been and continues to be rather a native state with wide fields of missionary work than an English settlement. According to the census of 1881, there were only 28,483 whites in a total population of 416,219. In 1837 a large number of Dutch farmers, irritated by the action of the British Government in repressing slavery, migrated from the Cape Colony to Natal. For two years they were engaged in war with Dingaarn, the Kafir chief, who had murdered his brother Chaka. The Dutch,

Natal

being at last victorious, deposed Dingaarn and made his brother Panda king. The British Government determined to annex the country, and in 1845 it became part of the Cape Colony, Roman Dutch law being established. In 1856 it became a separate colony, but already it had received its first bishop, the Rev. J. W. Colenso. With the exception possibly of Bishop Callaway, who accompanied Bishop Colenso to Africa, no missionary, whether bishop or priest, has so thoroughly sympathised with the Kafirs, has so entirely mastered their language and history, or has been so trusted and respected by them. Bishop Colenso saw at once that his labours among the colonists would not engross a large portion of his time and care. The English were numerically insignificant in proportion to the mass of heathens among whom they dwelt. Other missionary agencies were at work, from Scotland, from Holland, from America, from Germany, and from Rome; but the Church of England had as yet done nothing. He not only learned Kafir, but, by laboriously compiling a Zulu dictionary and grammar, he made it easier for others to learn it. He had several able and devoted colleagues, among whom was the Rev. C. F. Mackenzie, afterwards first bishop in Central Africa. Then came painful signs of a change in his theological opinions, which disturbed many minds at home and abroad. Into this controversy these pages will not further enter than to state historical facts. In 1863 he was deposed from his office by the bishops of South Africa assembled at Capetown; and on appeal the sentence was pronounced by the Judicial Committee of the Privy Council to be 'null

Bishop Colenso

and void in law.' The bishop therefore continued in undisturbed possession of his income until his death in 1883. His missionary work in the last twenty years of his life was very limited. He was without large funds, which are essential for the conduct of such work, and his following was small in number and generally not influential. To the end he continued to be the champion and friend of the Zulus; he stood between the Government and the natives, and often secured for the latter justice and sympathy. The Church of South Africa continued to affirm the spiritual validity of the sentence passed on the Bishop of Natal; and on the Conversion of St. Paul, 1869, the Rev. W. K. Macrorie was consecrated Bishop of Maritzburg. Few men have been placed in a position of greater difficulty and responsibility. Everything had to be begun anew, for the churches generally were vested in Bishop Colenso. New churches and schools, therefore, had to be built, and the missions had to be cherished and developed under the dispiriting influence of a divided Church. Nevertheless, with much patience and forbearance, the work was carried on, until the churches in connection with the South African Church in the colony and the clergy who served them, were about four times as numerous as those which acknowledged the authority of Bishop Colenso. The time has now come for the schism to be healed; many good men both in Africa and in England have endeavoured to effect so desirable a consummation, and that the breach may be mended must be the desire of all. The presence of more than 20,000 Indian coolies adds to the responsibilities of the Church in Natal.

Bishop Macrorie

North of the River Tugela lies Zululand, the scene of bloodshed in recent years. It seemed to Bishop Colenso, soon after his arrival in Africa, so promising a field of missionary work that he sought to relieve himself of Natal and to give all his energies to the field beyond. This, however, he could not accomplish; but, although it formed no part of his diocese he cared for it as though it were under his charge. In 1860 a mission party set out and crossed the Tugela. For 200 miles they travelled in their waggons, fording bridgeless rivers. Everywhere there were signs that the people were ground down by their rulers, and that witchcraft and superstition were dominant. The travellers found welcome and kindness at the stations which the Norwegian missionaries had established, and at last settled at a spot called Kwamagwaza, which King Panda had given them. The people periodically rebelled against their rulers, who in their turn governed with frightful severity and injustice. The missionaries had to steer a difficult course; they had to refrain from any complicity with either party, and yet they were bound to protest against what was cruel and unjust. In 1870 a bishop was consecrated for Zululand, and was received with cordiality by Panda and Cetewayo, his son and successor. In five years the see was again vacant, and in 1880, after an interregnum of five years, the Ven. Douglas McKenzie, who had been Archdeacon of Harrismith, was consecrated Bishop of Zululand. The history of this region since the Bishop's consecration has been a story of continued bloodshed and warfare, and the story of the mission is painfully affected by the condition of the country. The Bishop has led the life of a hunted hare. Frequent changes of government, and with every change a change of policy, the breakdown of what was called Sir Garnet Wolseley's 'settlement,' the open action and the secret treachery of the Boers, the internecine struggles of the chiefs, have kept the land in a condition always of unrest and often of danger. The missionaries have more than once had to cross into the colony for safety, and have returned almost before it was prudent to do so. The mission stations have been destroyed, and rebuilt, only to be destroyed again. And yet through the long series of disasters and sorrows, probably never equalled in other missions, the work has gone on, the schools maintained, worship regularly offered, and the bishop, by living much in the saddle, has kept all the scattered elements together, and made others as calm as himself.

In his long tour in 1850, Bishop Gray reached what was called 'the Sovereignty beyond the Orange River,' which had been peopled by the Dutch, who found there less restriction on their slave-keeping propensities than existed at the Cape. Here the Bishop found some English settlers, whom he encouraged to build a church. Archdeacon Merriman subsequently visited them, and laid the corner-stone of the Church of St. Andrew. But before the church could be finished the British Government abandoned the Sovereignty, and in March 28, 1854, the English chaplain left, having made the following entry in the registers of the Church: 'The Orange River territory abandoned by the English.' But the English settlers remained under the changed government, and were apparently

The Orange Free State

forgotten by the Church. Some joined the Wesleyans, some the Dutch Church, some the Roman Church, feeling that their own communion had deserted them. In 1863, the Propagation Society undertook to provide the maintenance of a bishop for the Free State, and the charge entrusted to him included the Transvaal and Basutoland. The Basutos live in small villages; the Barolongs prefer to settle in towns, and at Thaba 'Nchu there is a population of some 15,000 of them. To these districts have subsequently been added Griqualand West, and the newly acquired colony of Bechuanaland, the scene of the noble labours of the late Dr. Moffat, while a Bishop of Pretoria has taken charge of the Transvaal. The work of the Church in the diocese of Bloemfontein has been supported with very large funds from England; the work of ladies living in community has been its prominent feature, and their labours in hospital have been gratefully recognised. The old church of 1854 was rebuilt and solemnly consecrated as the Cathedral Church of St. Andrew. Another and larger cathedral has since been partially erected. A brotherhood, under the leadership of Canon Beckett, was established in 1867; and, after trying several localities, the community settled at Modderport, on two farms which they purchased. In 1878 the diocese of Pretoria, which was then the capital of a new colony, was made a bishop's see, and the Rev. H. B. Bousfield was consecrated first bishop. He found his diocese in a state of siege, for the Boers had risen against the British Government. After a short time the country was ceded and became once more a Dutch republic. There are about 3,000 English

Pretoria

people settled in the republic, but the Kafir population is estimated at 1,000,000, for whom the German missionaries have done much.

Twelve hundred miles distant from the coast of Africa in the direct course of the South Atlantic trade-wind, there lies the island of St. Helena, once a place of the highest importance as being in the direct route to India; now, by the formation of the Suez Canal and the consequent diversion of the route, almost bereft of trade and intercourse with the world. The bishopric, which was formed in 1859, includes the island of Ascension, 800 miles northward, and the island of Tristan d'Acunha, about 1,500 miles to the southward. Ascension is only a garrison and a sanatorium; in St. Helena the Church has worked with much blessing among the coloured population; and in Tristan d'Acunha, the loneliest outpost of the Church, a very singular community has received very special care at the hands of the Church. In 1816 this islet, just five miles square, was fortified by order of the Government, and a company of artillery was stationed there. In 1821, on the death of Napoleon, the soldiers were withdrawn; but a corporal named Glass, with his wife and two children and two comrades, six souls in all, were allowed to remain and to cultivate the soil. They traded with the whalers that touched at the island; some shipwrecked persons found a refuge among them, and gradually their number nearly reached a hundred souls. One or two clergymen, on their way to India, had in the course of twenty years landed and baptized the children and married several couples, the good old Corporal Glass continuing to exercise a sort of patri-

archal priesthood among the people. In 1851 the
Propagation Society sent out a young clergyman, who
A remote colony for five years ministered to the little flock,
holding daily school, and having among his
scholars persons whose ages varied from five to twenty-
five years. In 1856, Bishop Gray visited this, the most
inaccessible part of his diocese, and found that the
people were willing to leave it and to settle on the
mainland. Sir George Grey sent a ship of war to
fetch them away; but, at the last moment, thirty determined to remain. In 1867, when the Duke of
Edinburgh visited Tristan, he found that the population had again risen to eighty-five, who greatly desired
to have a clergyman with them. In 1881 the Propagation Society sent out the Rev. E. H. Dodgson, who
found a parish with 107 souls waiting to receive him;
but, after four years of very patient and isolated work,
he returned to represent to the Colonial Office the absolute necessity of removing the people from their barren
home and leaving the island to the penguins and other
sea-birds, for which alone it is adapted.

On the eastern coast of Africa there are two islands
which are scenes of important Church work; one is the
Mauritius colony of Mauritius, the other the large kingdom of Madagascar. Mauritius came to Great
Britain in 1814 from the French, and French it remains
to this day in language and in religion. The English
Government pledged itself to the maintenance of the
French ecclesiastical establishment which had existed
for a hundred years, and the English Church has been
the creed of only a small minority of the colonists.
Nominally attached to the diocese of Calcutta, no

English bishop ever landed on the island until Bishop Chapman, of Colombo, visited it in 1850, when he consecrated the churches and confirmed a number of persons.

But if the island is small, and the people largely alien in language and faith, the necessities of trade have *Its variety of peoples* made it one of the great mission-fields of the world. There are in the island about a quarter of a million of Hindoo, Tamil, or Telugu-speaking coolies, who come under engagement for five years, and then return to their homes. There is also a motley population of Africans, Malagache, Singhalese, Arabs, Malays, and Chinese. In the Seychelles there is a large African population which has been increased by bodies of slaves released from men-of-war. Of the eighteen clergymen in the diocese seven are natives.

The island of Madagascar is about the size of France and has a population, which is estimated at five millions. *Madagascar and its tribes* It is occupied by several races, of whom the Sakalava, supposed to be the original children of the soil, dwell within well-defined regions of their own. The Betsimisaraka, who dwell chiefly on the coast, are the lowest class, and are for the most part in a kind of slavery of the patriarchal type, while the Hovas, who are the dominant race, having invaded the country at a very early period of its history, occupy the high table-land in the interior. About 1820, Radama I., a chief of the Hovas, succeeded in subduing the several tribes and placing them under himself as supreme monarch. A clever and far-seeing man, he entered into friendly relations with England, who in return gave him some munitions of war and allowed some officers to go to Madagascar and drill his troops. On his death his queen, Ranavalona I., succeeded him; she dreaded the presence of foreigners and ordered all aliens out of the kingdom. This was followed by a most savage persecution of the native Christians, of which more will be written hereafter. In 1861 she was succeeded by her son, Radama II., who desired that peace and toleration should characterise his reign. He was a weak man and a drunkard, and after a year was murdered in the palace. His queen succeeded him, and her reign was uneventful. In 1868 she was succeeded by Ramona, who became Ranavalona II. At her coronation all heathen rites were absent. By the side of the throne was a table supporting a copy of the Malagasy Bible and the laws of the island, and on the canopy over the throne was inscribed 'Glory to God. Peace on earth, goodwill to men. God be with us.'

The credit of the first entrance into Madagascar with the message of the Gospel belongs to the Church of Rome, which sent missionaries about the year 1770. Being French, they experienced the jealousy and hatred with which the people regard everything connected with France, which, more than once or twice, has attempted to conquer the island, and has long held under treaty some ports on the western coast. They enjoyed the monopoly of the missionary power in the island until 1818, when the London Missionary Society sent fourteen teachers, who reduced the language to writing, translated much of the Scriptures, and built two chapels in the capital, besides establishing preaching stations elsewhere. Then, in 1828, came the edict which banished all foreigners; and the missionaries,

Earliest missions

French and English alike, had to leave. But they left behind them that which could not die. Their converts had not hitherto made ostentatious professions of Christianity, but persecution strengthened their faith. As soon as the teachers had left, the queen commanded all who had received baptism or had attended Christian worship or had observed Sunday as holy, to come forward within one month and acknowledge their acts, throwing themselves on the royal clemency. Great numbers confessed, and found the royal clemency to be cruel. Four hundred nobles were degraded, others were deprived of their rank in the army. It was then ordered that all books should be given up, the retention of a single leaf being regarded as a capital offence. Officers were sent into suspected districts, and all who were supposed to be Christians were commanded to abjure their faith. 'To change what the ancestors had ordered and done, and to pray to the ancestors of foreigners and not to Nampanimerina and Lehidama and the idols that sanctify the twelve kings and the twelve mountains that are worshipped, whosoever changes these observances I will kill, saith Ranavalona,' was the edict of this queen, and she kept her word. Many Christians were thrown from a rock, some were speared, not a few were crucified, some were sold into lifelong slavery. The details of the death and sufferings of these martyrs were recorded by their surviving brethren, and in the whole range of Christian martyrology there are few stories more affecting. Many, however, went into hiding and carried with them the precious copies of the Scriptures. On the death of the Queen in 1861, they came forth from

Persecution of Christians

the woods and the caves in which they had dragged out a miserable existence; and it was said that the number of Christians was greater when the Queen died than when she ascended the throne.

The Jesuits and the London Missionary Society's agents returned in force to the capital as soon as the land was opened. Bishop Ryan, of Mauritius, was present at the king's coronation, and was invited by Radama II. to send missionaries to the capital. The London Missionary Society desired to keep the Church of England out of the capital; but in 1864 the Propagation Society and the Church Missionary Society each sent two missionaries, who were stationed on the coast. It was soon found that a mission not represented at the capital and recognised there by the dominant Hovas would not commend itself even to the lower and enslaved races. In spite of the faithful testimony which persecution had drawn out, it was evident that four-fifths of the population were still heathen, that trial by Tangena or the ordeal of poison was in full force, and that among the nominal Christians there was much immorality and superstition. The land therefore was open to all, and there need be no fear of inter-proselytism between Christian bodies. In 1872 the Rev. A. Chiswell, worn out by the fever and ague of the coast, went to the capital for change of air. He took with him seven boys, whom he was training to be themselves teachers, and with these and a few other Church folk, whom business had taken to the capital, he held service in his hired house. Gradually others sought admission, or stood at the open doors, and he put up a little church and schoolhouse, which was

The island reopened

opened, according to the custom of the country, in the presence of the Queen's representatives. This led the way to a larger church, and ultimately to a bishop being sent to direct the whole mission. In 1874 the Rev. R. K. Kestell-Cornish was consecrated, on the request of the Archbishop of Canterbury, by the bishops of the Scottish Church in Edinburgh. The Church Missionary Society at this time transferred their Madagascar missionaries to Japan, and the Propagation Society has since maintained all the missionaries of the English Church in the island. The apprehensions of the Independents have been shown to themselves to have been illusory, for the bishop and his clergy have joined with them in the work of translation; and, while each party has kept to its own proper work, the personal relations of the members of both missions have been characterised by mutual respect and courtesy. The work of the Church at Antananarivo, the capital, with its population of 100,000, and its numberless villages within a radius of a dozen miles, has been to raise a high Christian standard of life, devotion, and worship, and to train native catechists and clergymen, who shall be planted out in different parts of the island, when they shall have proved their competence and trustworthiness. In the Theological College, erected by the Rev. F. A. Gregory, a day's journey from the capital, a general and theological education is given, which embraces all the elements of a really liberal education, and so popular is the institution that entrance is obtained now after competitive examinations, whereas in its earlier days young men had to be invited and almost coaxed to enter. The

An English bishop sent out

Prospects of an indigenous clergy

work (and no portion of missionary work is more important) of training the girls and women in decent and thrifty domestic habits, has received great attention, one lady, Miss Lawrence, having from the first won the hearts of the people to whom she has given her own and many years of devoted labour. Of the fourteen missionaries who occupy the capital and its adjacent villages, and three very important centres on the coast, five are natives. The attack which France so wantonly made on the east coast of Madagascar sadly hindered the progress of the country; but the mission work was hardly checked, although the missionaries were exposed to many privations, and in some cases to danger. The Rev. James Coles heroically held to his post at Tamatave all through the siege of that port, and his courage was recognised and appreciated by the French officers, who showed him many kindnesses. At Mahonoro a shell carried away the roof of Miss Lawrence's house, where she was calmly doing her work. Moreover, the difficulty of obtaining money and supplies from England affected all English alike; but, as has been already stated, there has been no direct interference with spiritual work. With the first appearance of the French fleet on the coast, the Jesuit missionaries realised their danger. They were ordered to leave the country, but they never expected to make the ten days' journey to the coast without being attacked. Bishop Kestell-Cornish represented to the authorities that the customs of civilised warfare demanded that they should be sent with all safety and consideration to the coast, and the French priests have been forward to

marginal note: The French blockade

acknowledge that for their safety, and possibly for their lives, they were indebted to the good offices of the English bishop.

CHAPTER XI.

MISSIONS ON THE EASTERN COAST OF AFRICA.

THE Church Missionary Society, whose connection with the west coast of Africa is a very glorious record of missionary work, has also the distinction of having been the first agency of the Church to break ground on the eastern coast. In 1815 it attempted to assist the Abyssinian Church to reform itself, and Dr. Gobat, afterwards bishop in Jerusalem, resided in Abyssinia from 1830 to 1833; and Dr. Krapf from 1839 to 1842. Dr. Krapf was much interested in the Somali and Galla tribes, and, finding himself at Zanzibar in 1854, he received from the Imam of Muscat a letter of safe-conduct to all the governors of the eastern coast, in which he was described as ' a good man who wishes to convert the world to God.' At length he settled himself at Mombasa, a small island separated from the eastern coast of Africa only by a shallow ford. Here was a busy centre of trade, and a very mixed population of 12,000 souls. He had hardly begun his work here when his wife died, but his solitary condition in no degree suggested to him that he should retire. On the contrary, he wrote to the Society : ' Here on the East African coast is the lonely grave of one of your friends,

The Church Missionary Society's early work in Africa

a sign that you have commenced the struggle with this part of the world.' He was joined by Dr. Rebmann in 1845, who gave thirty years of toil to the mission. They made long journeys into the interior, and were the first white men to discover Kilimanjaro, the now well-known snow-capped mountain of 20,605 feet altitude. Sickness and death reduced the mission staff, until Rebmann was the solitary member remaining, and he was driven away in 1856 by a hostile tribe. He went to Zanzibar, and there diligently arranged all the materials which he had gathered for compiling vocabularies and making translations in three distinct languages. After three years he returned, and, finding a warm welcome, he continued at Mombasa until 1875.

Meantime the revelations which were made of the increasing atrocities of the slave trade called for vigorous action on the part of the Government. Livingstone had testified to the impossibility of exaggerating its enormities, and in 1872 the late Sir Bartle Frere was sent to Zanzibar and Madagascar on a special embassy. The Society felt bound to enlarge its work in these regions, and by the transfer from India of some liberated Africans, who had been under Christian training at Nassick, an industrial Christian colony was formed, to which many additions have been made, as slaves have been landed from ships of war. The mission at Mombasa has done service far beyond its own limits. The dictionaries and grammars of the older missionaries have been of inestimable value to those who have laboured on other parts of the coast; and, but for the labours of these pioneers, it is improbable that the very successful venture which the same Society

The slave trade

has made in the interior and on Lake Nyanza could have been carried out as it has been.

For the sake of chronological order a mission far to the south of Mombasa must next be noticed. In 1856, Livingstone, having spent sixteen years in Africa and published the result of his labours and travels, threw down a challenge to the Christian world in the words: 'I regard the geographical feat as the beginning of the missionary enterprise.' He appealed immediately to the English universities; but his appeal fell dead, and he returned to Africa having apparently accomplished nothing. But in 1859 Bishop Gray took up the story, and the two universities were persuaded to accept the challenge. This was done to a partial extent only. The universities of Oxford, Cambridge, Dublin, and Durham gave their names to a new missionary society which was then founded, not without frequent declarations on the part of its founders that it was to exist only for a short time and then to be merged in an older organisation; but, as was natural, money was raised in all parts, and only a small proportion came from the universities. Probably the secret of the enthusiasm with which the work was commenced was that there had been forthcoming, just at the critical moment, the natural leader of the expedition. Archdeacon Mackenzie had just returned from Natal, to make preparations for a mission to Zululand. To him the call was made, and in his own modest way he at once obeyed. Leaving England in the autumn of 1860, he was consecrated in Capetown on January 1, 1861, and immediately left, with three priests, a lay superintendent, a carpenter, a labourer, and three native converts, who had been educated at Capetown. The mouth of the Zambesi River, which was the natural approach to their destination, was the beginning of their troubles. By Livingstone's advice, they attempted the shallower Rovuma and found progress impossible. The Zambesi, to which they had to return, was now shallower than when first attempted; and after eight toilsome weeks the party reached a point called 'Chibisas,' whence they started on foot for the higher lands on which they hoped to settle. At last, not without collisions with slave-dealers, Livingstone left them at Magomero, 4,000 feet above the sea, with some rescued slaves on whom to begin their work of education. But the site was not a healthy one. Fever was generally present, and an exceptional and unprecedented famine visited the country. Reinforcements came to the mission, but only to fall victims to the fever. The bishop, who had gone to meet a new-comer, the Rev. H. Burrup, was thrown into the water by the capsizing of his canoe; and on January 31, 1862, just thirteen months after his consecration, he breathed his last on the lonely island of Malo, where his grave for many years called on the English Church to occupy the continent, but called in vain. In February, 1863, his successor was consecrated, and in May he arrived at the mouth of the Zambesi. There he learned that only three Englishmen of the original party were alive. On reaching Magomero he was advised by the old missionaries to move to a spot twenty miles away; but he decided to occupy Morumbala. This was soon abandoned, together with the people whom the older

First settlement

The Bishop's death

missionaries had won, and whose confidence they had gained. In 1864 Bishop Tozer sent to England the mechanics whom he had taken out, and decided to establish himself at Zanzibar. Before the mission on the mainland was utterly broken up, some of the women and about twenty boys were taken to the Cape; others were entrusted to the care of the Ajawa tribe, and, as it turned out, with much sound judgment, for in the first Livingstone Search Expedition of 1867 it was found that they were living together in peace and comfort, dwelling much on the teaching of their 'English Fathers,' and expecting their return. Meanwhile the interest in the mission, now transferred to Zanzibar, languished and died. The bishop was educating a few lads given to him by the Sultan; but it was felt that the great promise of the original venture of Bishop Mackenzie had dwindled to something extremely small, and so funds failed as interest and hope failed. The mission had to draw on its capital; its home expenses were high, and the secretary reported to the committee in 1866 that 'he had been obliged almost entirely to abandon the attempt to organise meetings, owing to the great expense attending them; that collections and offertories had fallen from 1,109*l*. in 1864 to 380*l*. in 1866; while subscriptions had fallen below 400*l*. per annum; that Dublin had withdrawn; that Durham had sent no contribution; and that both at Oxford and Cambridge he was told that 40*l*. or 50*l*. was the utmost that could be expected.' Thus in about six years utter collapse had followed a bright promise. The bishop returned to England and by his presence raised a considerable sum of money. Finding that large home expenditure had hitherto failed in raising an income that would justify its continuance, he determined to throw the fortunes of the mission on the voluntary efforts of its friends; but five years' experience showed that the plan was unpractical, and a paid home organisation was again resolved upon. This, combined with efforts abroad to carry out the original plan of the mission, revived interest, and the income of the mission is on a scale which does full credit to its supporters.

But while things were critical at home they were in even worse plight in Zanzibar. When Sir Bartle Frere visited the eastern coast of Africa in 1873, he made a careful inspection of all the missionary agencies at work in those regions. He found Dr. Steere in Zanzibar the solitary ordained missionary. Several valuable lives had been lost: the climate of Zanzibar, which had been declared by Captain Burton to be very unhealthy, was now in worse odour than ever, but Sir Bartle Frere expressed his belief that its unhealthiness had been much exaggerated, and he wrote to the Archbishop of Canterbury in the following words: 'The same might have been said of India till we found out how to live there and to preserve health. I am sure that no men could live in India as I saw some of my countrymen living in Zanzibar, with such disregard of exposure and neglect of sanitary precautions, without losing health and often life.' Meanwhile Dr. Steere's industry at the work of translation, which had been commenced by Krapf and Rebmann, was producing results which would have their value when evangelistic work should be resumed in earnest. A station at

Threatened collapse at home and abroad

Magila on the mainland had been opened by the Rev. C. A. Alington in 1867; but he had been called to England by a summons which he could not disobey, and the post had come to be held by a young layman, and was only a pledge of future work. Other bodies had in the meantime established themselves on the continent. The Free Kirk of Scotland had actually occupied a station known as Livingstonia, on the Lake Nyassa, the goal of Bishop Mackenzie's party which they had failed to reach; and the Established Church of Scotland had founded the station of Blantyre, on the Shiré Highlands, close to the very spot on which Bishop Mackenzie had resided.

Presbyterian missions on mainland

In 1874, on the consecration of Bishop Steere, the prospects of the mission at once brightened. Starting from Lindi, about 400 miles south of Zanzibar, he established a party, chiefly composed of released slaves who had been trained at Zanzibar, at Masasi, 130 miles inland, and on the road to Lake Nyassa. The Rev. W. P. Johnson subsequently established a mission, 250 miles beyond Masasi, at Mwembe, in the Ajawa country, where he secured the good-will of the chief Mataka. Archdeacon Farler from Magila has developed the work in the Usambara country, where there are five stations. It is difficult to discover the number of baptized converts, whether among the rescued slaves or the natives; but it has been stated that not fewer than 800 natives of the country are 'under the influence of the mission.' After Bishop Steere's death in August 1882 great difficulty was experienced in finding a suitable successor, till in 1884

Bishop Steere recommences work on the mainland

the Rev. C. A. Smythies was consecrated the fourth Bishop of Central Africa.

On Lake Tanganyika, which until Burton and Speke's expedition of 1857 was supposed to be part of Lake Nyanza, the London Missionary Society has an extensive mission under whose auspices a road has been made connecting the two lakes.

Lake Tanganyika

It now remains to describe the very gallant occupation by the Church Missionary Society of the great lake Victoria Nyanza, which lies on the equator. In 1857 Captains Burton and Speke saw only the southern end of Lake Nyanza, and it was not until 1861 that Captain Speke, in company with Captain Grant, fully explored the lake and telegraphed to England the brief but significant message ' *The Nile is settled.*' Captain Speke claimed but a modest share of the credit of this discovery. He wrote: 'The missionaries are the prime and first promoters of this discovery. They have been for years doing their utmost, with simple sincerity, to Christianise this negro land. They heard from Arabs and others of a large lake or inland sea, and they very naturally, and I may add, fortunately, put upon the map that monster slug of an inland sea, which so much attracted the attention of the geographical world in 1855-6 and caused our being sent out to Africa.' In 1864 Sir Samuel Baker discovered the smaller equatorial lake which lies further to the westward and is called the Albert Nyanza.

Lake Nyanza

In 1874 Mr. H. M. Stanley circumnavigated the Victoria Nyanza and had an interview with King Mtesa, who had previously received Speke and Grant. He found him no longer a rude savage,

Mr. H. M. Stanley and King Mtesa

but earnest in his profession of Mohammedanism. Mr. Stanley recounted, in a letter which appeared in the *Daily Telegraph* of November 15, 1876, his experiences with the king, and assured the English people that Mtesa was willing to receive and protect Christian teachers. The story seemed to many incredible; others thought that the king had deceived Mr. Stanley by fair words; to others happily it appeared a providential opening. Three days after the letter had appeared, the Church Missionary Society received an offer of 5,000*l*. towards the cost of a mission to the Victoria Nyanza. Another offer of an equal amount was made within a few days; and the Society, thus encouraged, determined to establish a mission in an almost unknown country, 800 miles from the coast. In 1877 the first exploring party under the leadership of Lieutenant Shergold Smith, R.N., reached the lake, and found the king as good as his word, but soon afterwards a dispute, caused by an Arab trader who had fled to the mission party for protection, caused them to be attacked and all but one were killed. In the early part of the next year the mission was established at Mpwapwa about 150 miles from the coast, and from thence it was determined without delay to push onwards, the stations on the route being regarded at first only as resting-places, although they have since become centres of light and sources of Christian influences to the tribes around. In 1884 the Rev. J. Hannington, who two years before had led a party to Mpwapwa, was consecrated Bishop of Eastern Equatorial Africa, and a boat named the 'Eleanor' was launched on the waters of the Lake Victoria Nyanza, while on the coast the missionary

<small>The C. M. S. mission to Lake Nyanza.</small>

steamer 'Henry Wright' is at the service of the party. The bishop found himself at the head of a mission which had five stations, thirteen European missionaries, and sixty-eight native Christians, of whom forty were communicants. It is not pretended that the spiritual hindrances to the Gospel in these regions are to be compared with those which confront the evangelist in India. There are no caste prejudices, no systems of faith crystallised by the observance of many generations; but with all these deductions it may reasonably be doubted whether in so short a time as seven years from the despatch of the first exploring party a mission has ever been so wisely and successfully planted in its integrity as has been the mission to the Victoria Nyanza.

<small>Progress</small>

In 1884 King Mtesa died, not ignorant of Christianity, but not having been baptized. It was feared that his removal might place the mission in danger, but, for the time at least, the influence of the missionaries prevailed with the people, and the slaughter which commonly marks the decease of an African monarch, was not allowed.

<small>Death of King Mtesa</small>

But the fair prospect was soon clouded. Mwanga, the new king, dreaded the increase of Europeans in his country, and was jealous of the missionaries' influence. In October 1885 Bishop Hannington determined to go to Uganda by a new and short route. When within about four days' journey from Uganda, he and his fifty companions were seized and imprisoned; further instructions were awaited by the captors, and the order at length came from the king that they were to be executed. The news that this

<small>Murder of mission party</small>

dread sentence had been carried out, only four of the party having escaped, reached England on New Year's Day 1886. The hope that there might be some exaggeration was cherished, but there seems to be little doubt that the good bishop's career ended in a death that may be called sacrificial in its character.

A glance at the map of Africa is or ought to be, a strong stimulant of missionary zeal; whatever may be the fortune of the continent in regard to material things, it is at present a large blank in the map of spiritual adventure. Somalis and Gallas in vast numbers occupy the territory between Mombasa and Aden, the natural centre of evangelistic work both in Arabia and in Abyssinia. The corrupt Churches of Egypt and Abyssinia, and the absolute effacement by the power of Islam of the Churches of North Africa, these present problems to be dealt with only by men of profound wisdom and charity. On the Western Coast, as the next chapter will show, much has been done; and, as though to stir up the energies which may be content to rest with the accomplishments of the past, Mr. H. M. Stanley reports a residence of six years on the river Congo, during which stations have been established on its banks for the purposes of trade for 1,500 miles from the coast. With the opening of the country lying between the Soudan and the equator the whole continent will have been made known to the world, and it will be for the Church to cross and recross it in divers directions with chains of mission stations.

Prospects of missions in Central Africa

CHAPTER XII.

MISSIONS ON THE WESTERN COAST OF AFRICA.

SIERRA LEONE, to which country has been given the ill-sounding name of 'the white man's grave,' has the high honour of being the scene of noble devotion and prodigality of life in the cause of Christianity unparalleled in any other part of the world. Desolated for many generations by the atrocities of the slave trade, its very misfortunes led to its first being cared for by philanthropic men. In 1787, Granville Sharpe procured the settlement on the peninsula of Sierra Leone of a number of released slaves who were living in great indigence and misery in the streets of London. Four years later, Wilberforce and his friends obtained for the Sierra Leone Company possession of the peninsula, and of several forts and factories along the Gold Coast. In 1804 the Church Missionary Society sent its agents to Western Africa; in 1808, Sierra Leone became a British colony, and the Government having in the previous year abolished slavery throughout the British dominions, the living cargoes of the slave-ships which English cruisers captured became free on their landing on English territory.

First settlement

Into this colony there were gathered members of various tribes, more than one hundred in number, speaking widely different languages: it was therefore found necessary to make English the common medium of instruction. For it soon became apparent that only by a native ministry could the Church be maintained in regions so fatal to the European. In the first twenty years of the existence of the mission fifty-three missionaries or missionaries' wives died at their posts. In 1823, out of five missionaries who went out, four died within six months; in the next year six volunteers were accepted and of them two died within four months of their landing. These losses seemed but to draw out more zeal, for in the next year three more went forth, of whom two died within six months; but neither then nor at any subsequent time has there been any difficulty in filling up the ranks of the West African Mission.

Mortality of white people

In 1852 Sierra Leone became a diocese, but the first three bishops—Vidal, Weeks, and Bowen—died within eight years of the creation of the see. The Church has now become self-supporting and self-expanding; the whole of the pastoral work is in the hands of an indigenous clergy, and the educational institutions have supplied evangelists and teachers for the regions beyond.

The episcopate

Foremost among the extensions of the Sierra Leone Church must be placed the Yoruba and the Niger missions, 1,300 miles to the eastward. For generations the people groaned under the burdens of their rulers, who contended with each other for the privilege of selling the people into slavery. About the year 1820, a small company of Yorubans fled for shelter to the desert, and many others joined them in their comparative safety. Obliged for reasons of self-preservation to enlarge their borders and to seek a wider field, they ventured into the hill-country and there built huts

Yoruba and the Niger

and cultivated the soil. At length the refugees of 130 towns were collected together; they built villages, which they named after the places which they had left, and the whole colony they called Abbeokuta. In thirty years they became a peaceful and industrious but heathen community of 80,000 souls, sacrificing human victims to the blood-thirsty deities whom their own imaginations had created. Among them were some Yorubans, who on their release from the grasp of the slave-dealer had imbibed some Christian teaching at Sierra Leone, and thence had returned to their own land. They were in their measure and degree missionaries to their brethren; their report of English kindness and love prompted the colony to send to Sierra Leone a request for teachers. A young catechist, Mr. Townsend, visited them; and two years later, having been meanwhile ordained, he returned with two other clergymen. Now the powers of evil were active; persecution was resorted to; the tyrannical kings of the adjacent country of Dahomey interfered; in 1867 all the churches, with a single exception, were despoiled, worship was forbidden, and the missionaries, driven out of the country, found refuge at Lagos; but the first to return was a native priest. One of the churches was rebuilt as a solemn act of expiation, and Christianity revived in greater vigour than it had ever previously shown.

Abbeokuta

So long ago as 1841 the British Government sent three ships of war to open the regions of the River Niger to legitimate commerce. They carried with them a clergyman attached to the Church Missionary Society's staff in Sierra Leone, and Mr. Crowther, a lay-teacher, who had been a slave. The expedition was doomed to be a conspicuous failure, 42 out of 150 white men, who were engaged in it, having died in sixty-two days. The clergyman, however, managed to pick up enough of the Hausa language to enable him with further study to translate portions of the Old and New Testament into that tongue, which is one of the most widely-spread of African languages. The Christian negroes who had accompanied him joined with him, on his return, in the assurance that the land was open to the Gospel. Another expedition in 1854 penetrated 500 miles into the interior, and in 1857 yet another expedition was sent. Mr. Crowther, who had meanwhile been ordained, remained behind and established himself at Onitsha, where the first mission was formed. Mohammedanism and its accompanying slave trade hindered the work in many ways; but the progress of the mission, which from the first has been conducted wholly by native clergymen and teachers, has been continuous and eventful. Stranger than the wildest dreams of fiction has been the career of Mr. Crowther. Born in slavery, he was bartered as a lad in exchange for a horse, and was returned on his owner's hands as an unfair bargain. On two subsequent occasions he was exchanged for rum and tobacco respectively. In his hopeless misery he tried by suicide to put an end to an existence which was a protracted burthen. Sold to Portuguese traders, and from them rescued by an English cruiser, he was landed at Sierra Leone a free man. Here and in England he was educated by the Church Missionary Society, and he went with Mr. Townsend to Abbeokuta

Rev. S. (afterwards Bishop) Crowther

Mohammedan cruelty

in 1845. At that spot he met with his mother and sisters, from whom he had been separated for many years, and he led them to embrace Christianity. In 1857 he went to the Niger, and in 1864 was consecrated, in Canterbury Cathedral, bishop of the mission of which he had been the founder.

Islam still holds possession of the land, and among the pagan tribes is constantly making raids and carrying away the people as slaves. The hope of the country centres in the bishop and his twelve native clergymen. A steamer, known as the 'Henry Venn,' enables the bishop to visit the various stations on the river at all times of the year. Industrial schools are doing their work. The plough is bringing the soil under cultivation, and the mendicancy of Mohammedanism is giving way to self-respect and honest labour.

Between Sierra Leone and the Gold Coast there lie the American republic of Liberia and the independent colony of Maryland or Cape Palmas. In 1821 the American Colonisation Society established the republic of Liberia, as an outlet for free blacks, who enjoyed but a limited amount of independence in the United States, in consequence of local prejudices too strong to be eradicated. It was hoped, too, both that the policy of manumission would be encouraged, and that the new colony would carry civilisation and Christianity to the 30,000 negroes in the country. In 1835 the American Church established a mission at Cape Palmas, and in 1851 a resident bishop headed the work. The climate proved to be a very great hindrance, and made evident the necessity of committing the work at the

<small>Liberia and Maryland</small>

earliest possible date to natives of the country. The first bishop was no novice; he had laboured in the colony for fourteen years before he was called to the episcopate, and his whole service extended over thirty-four years. To Bishop Payne succeeded another labourer of long standing in the field. Bishop Auer was marked out by his conspicuous services for the vacant post. He was summoned to America for consecration, and he returned to Africa only to die. He held one confirmation, ordained two priests, and before the dawn of the next day had passed to his reward. The third bishop, Penick, who had been rector of a church in Baltimore, thought that the time had come when the work in the malarious districts might be entrusted to natives, and he established himself on the hills. After six years he resigned, his health proving that he was unfitted for the work, and in 1885 he was succeeded by Bishop Ferguson, a native Liberian, whose life has been spent in the country. The whole staff of the present mission—bishop, priests, and lay-teachers—are natives either of Liberia or of Maryland, and are inured to the climate and its peculiarities.

The American Church Mission

Yet another mission on the Western Coast of Africa demands notice, and it is of peculiar interest, in that it originated, not in England, but with the daughter Church of the West Indies. In 1851 the Rev. R. Rawle, the Principal of Codrington College, Barbados, made an appeal to the West Indian Church for Africa. 'We want,' he wrote, 'to leaven the West Indian dioceses with missionary feeling. We wish to make it a part of everyone's religion—in a population mainly derived from Africa, and, where not

The Pongas Mission

so derived, deeply indebted to Africa, by wrongs inflicted and by benefits obtained—to help in Africa's conversion. A great reaction is to be stirred up, opposite in direction as in character to the traffic by which these colonies were peopled, sending back to Africa, as missionaries, the descendants of those who were brought over here as slaves.' On June 16 of that year, the 'West Indian Church Society for the furtherance of the Gospel in Western Africa' was founded in Barbados. The other West Indian dioceses joined in the undertaking, and some help came from England, where a Corresponding Committee exists. In 1854 the first offer of personal service was made. A Barbadian clergyman, of more than middle age, regarded the death of his wife as a call to him to devote the rest of his life to Africa. Landing with Bishop Weeks at Sierra Leone in December, 1855, Mr. Leacock had no fixed plans, and left the scene of his work to be decided for him. The captain of H.M.S. 'Myrmidon' suggested to him the country round the Pongas river, about a hundred and fifty miles north of Sierra Leone. This seemed a providential opening, and Mr. Leacock was landed at the mouth of the Pongas, and commended by the captain to the good offices of the king, who promised fairly. But when the ship of war had steamed away, Mr. Leacock and his lay companion found that everything was changed. The Mohammedan chiefs warned the king that the presence of missionaries would injure the slave trade, and the king lent a ready ear to their counsels. No children came to school, and as the poor teacher lay sick on his bed in a miserable hut, hands and feet swollen with mosquito-bites, he saw his few possessions pilfered by the people, while he was impotent to interfere. Things were truly at a low point of hope, and, just when despair was winning the day, a strange visitor came to the hut. This was a young man, Lewis Wilkinson, son of a chief of Fallangia, bringing an invitation from his father. Ill as he was, Mr. Leacock went with him, and, to his surprise, was welcomed with absolute reverence by the chief, who with much emotion recited the *Te Deum*. The explanation was forthcoming, and the story was a strange one. The old chief had spent some of his early years in England, and in the family of a clergyman. Returning to Africa in 1813, he had gradually relapsed into heathenism. After many years a severe illness reminded him of his baptism, and of the higher teaching which he had received; and for twenty subsequent years, with much remorse, he had been endeavouring to recover what once he had learned, and his daily prayer had been that a missionary might be sent to him. Now, in Mr. Leacock's arrival he saw the answer to his prayer, and he could not do enough to show his gratitude. He immediately gave him the best lodging that was available, and he gave a piece of land, on which, by the liberality of the Churches of America and England, a mission-house was built. Mr. Leacock died in 1856, after repeated attacks of fever. Several who had volunteered died at their posts; and it was found necessary to allow only Africans or West Indians to join the work. At present the four clergymen who occupy Domingia, Fallangia, Farringia, and the Isles des Los, are all of negro race, and have been educated at Codrington College, Barbados. Not only have they done much spiritual work, but they have also introduced

[margin: Chief Wilkinson]

a higher civilisation and peaceful industry. Factories and printing-presses are doing their work in the land, and the people have been taught to grow cotton with more success, and to dress it by machinery, until it commands its price in the English market. The old chief Wilkinson died in 1861, but his sons continued the protection and sympathy which he consistently gave to the mission. The present condition of the mission is critical. What was possible to be done has been done. The Prayer Book and the New Testament have been translated into Susu; many hundreds of converts have been won. Meanwhile, France on one hand, and Germany on the other, are looking wistfully at adjacent territory, with a view to annexation. It is felt that the little band of missionaries should no longer be left without a head, and a proposal to establish a missionary bishop on the Pongas has been laid before the Church.

Christianity and civilisation

CHAPTER XIII.

MISSIONS IN THE EAST INDIES.

FROM the time of Herodotus downwards, what is now known as 'the Eastern question' has occupied the attention of the nations of the West, and history shows that the nations which in succession have been the link between the East and the West have for the time being risen to the height of opulence and influence. Arabia, Tyre, Alexandria, and Rome in the earliest times; Venice and Genoa in the middle ages;

Successive rulers of India

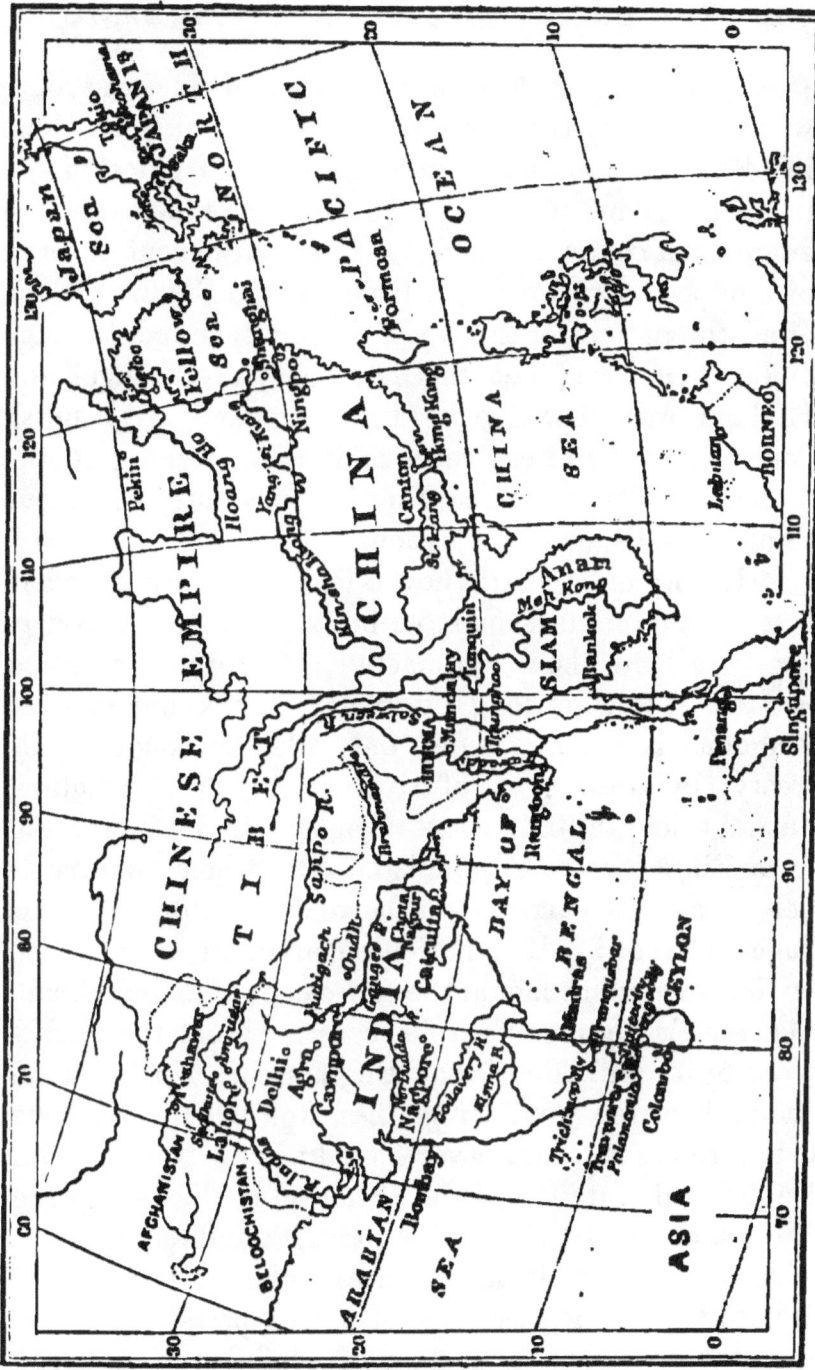

Portugal, Holland, France, and England since the route was diverted by the discovery of the Cape of Good Hope in 1498—each in their turn have found in Hindostan and in its abundant natural products a wide field for the energies of commerce, and for the enlargement of their own importance. Portugal, Holland, and England, alone of all the nations of the world, have attempted to make India their own; but the supremacy of Portugal and Holland was short-lived. India is now an English dependency; in direct revenue it adds nothing to the nation's wealth, yet of nothing is the country so jealous as of its undisputed possession.

How we obtained it; how a little company of traders first settled on its shores, without possessing a rood of land; how settlements were formed here and there at long intervals; how kingdom after kingdom has come under our rule, by conquest, by treaty, by dissensions of rival rulers, by annexation, until at length, from Cape Comorin to Peshawar and from Singapore to Afghanistan, the whole country is held as a huge garrison—is beyond the scope of these pages to record. If a nation's conscience is governed by the rules which mould the conscience of an individual, the story is not a subject for boasting; but the verdict of posterity will admit that England has conferred on India, however won, many blessings which under its native rulers it would never have known. Not only has English rule introduced the advanced civilisation of the West, and covered the land with canals and railways and telegraphic wires; it has given to India the treasures of literature, and the blessings of a free press, and it has established an equable system of administration under

English possession of India

laws to the making of which the natives themselves contribute. But the highest gifts, the truest civilisation, it could not give. When England first acquired supremacy in India, the time had not gone by when Governments were wont to undertake the task of evangelisation. It was ever a work requiring more delicate machinery than the edicts of Emperors or the bulls of Popes; and whatever England might have done or desired to do in this regard a hundred years ago, our religious divisions make impossible now. But what Governments cannot do is all the more incumbent on the Church, and it is to the credit of the consciences of Christian people, in America and in Germany as well as in Great Britain, that from the first they have recognised in India the field of special difficulty and the scene of noblest effort.

The first contact between India and Christianity occurred long ago. In apostolic times, or in the period immediately following, the disciples of St. Thomas, if not the apostle himself, made numerous converts among the Jewish communities, who had settled in India before the invasion of Alexander, and the heathen of Southern India, who were driven by persecution to take refuge in Travancore. A church which derives its bishops from the patriarchs of Babylon and Antioch has existed in Malabar for more than 1,500 years, and, so long ago as the ninth century of our era, obtained from native princes certain concessions and privileges. From time to time the Churches of Europe and Western Asia sent missionaries to the East. The Scriptures found a place in more than one Oriental library; and the Malabar Christians, free

Early converts to Christianity in India

from distinctly Roman theology until the arrival of the Portuguese, welcomed their Western visitors as brethren. Some sixty years later, when the Portuguese were expelled from India, the congregations on the coast were absorbed into the Church of Rome, while the congregations of the interior asserted their independence.

After Xavier, the next evangelist of note was Ziegenbalg; and the Danish missions rendered conspicuous service in Southern India. But Denmark was a poor country, and England gave money to their missions; on Ziegenbalg's death, funds from Denmark failed, and the Danish missions were adopted by the Society for Promoting Christian Knowledge, until in 1824 they were transferred to the Society for the Propagation of the Gospel. Schwartz has the credit of founding the first non-Roman mission in Tinnevelly. When he died, in 1798, he could point to hundreds of converts, to a higher tone in the administration of justice, and to respect which was accorded to himself by rajahs as well as by the poorest of their subjects. Then towards the close of the last century, Carey, a Baptist shoemaker from Northamptonshire, reached Calcutta and was soon followed by Marshman and three friends. The Government, alarmed at the arrival of so large a body, ordered them to re-embark, and they took refuge in the Danish mission at Serampore, where they laboured hard at the work of translating, printing, teaching, and preaching. When Lord Wellesley required a Bengali scholar to teach in the newly established college at Fort William, he had to ask the missionary whom the Government had banished from

[margin: Danish missions]

[margin: Serampore Baptist mission]

Calcutta some years before to accept the post. Carey lived on until 1834; but long before his death he had kindled the fire of missionary zeal in England and in America.

It must be acknowledged that until the year 1813 the missionary work that had been done in India had been the work of bodies not in communion with the national Church. Even the missionaries who were supported by Church Societies were in Lutheran orders. Several of the chaplains of the East India Company had contributed their share to the work; but their numbers were quite unequal to the task of ministering to the servants of the Company. Some of them did good service in making known to Parliament and to the world the horrors of heathenism, which then prevailed in the country; but it was not until 1814, when the East India Company's new charter made the country open to the Christian teacher, that the first actual missionary in Anglican orders was sent to India.

<small>English Church missions</small>

Let us attempt to understand what is the nature of the work of a missionary in India, what the country is like, who are the people, and what are the foremost hindrances in the way. India is not a homogeneous country, as people are prone to think. It is not one nation, but a *congeries* of nations differing one from another in character, in language, and in physique quite as widely as an Englishman differs from a Pole, or a Russian from a Spaniard, and occupying a seventh portion of the globe. They possess literature, sacred books, poems, philosophic treatises, and legends, whose massiveness is appalling. To the lack

<small>Conditions of missionary work in India</small>

of cohesion among these nations of varied creeds and languages we probably owe our retention of the land; but these many diversities add infinitely to the difficulties of the Evangelist. The mere thought of the babel of tongues is enough to appal the bravest. Excluding English, the language of the Government and of the highest education, which is rapidly becoming the language of educated India; excluding Sanskrit, the literary language of the Brahmans and other Indo-Aryans; excluding Persian, the literary language of the Mohammedans; excluding the languages spoken on the further side of the Indian frontier, such as Beluchi on the north-west, and the Burmese dialects on the eastern side of the Bay of Bengal, the languages spoken within the limits of India proper are not fewer than one hundred in number. About one-fifth of these are cultivated, writes Bishop Caldwell, but they are all capable of being used for the highest purpose to which a language can be applied—the conveying of the message of God's love to the soul and the soul's returning answer of grateful love. It is probable that in time the larger number of the people of the East may be reached by English, as the knowledge of it spreads through the land by means of the schools which the Government so liberally encourages. The process will not be without its disadvantages; the people will be strange to its idioms; and the preachers, untrained in the modes of thought and expression natural to the people, will not be in fullest sympathy with their intelligences. For the present, however, as in the past, the duty of the Church is to recognise the fact that, wherever a people speak a

Varieties of race and language

language of their own not understood by their neighbours, there is required a Bible, school-books, and, at least, the elements of a literature in the tongue which they understand.

In the northern region, of which Peshawar is the capital, two millions speak the Pashtu language. In Cashmere, where by the jealousy of its rulers, missionary work has been much hindered, the vernacular is spoken by a million and a half of people. In Thibet, where Hinduism begins to be supplanted by Buddhism, and where on the north the Russian Church has a mission and the Moravians have a station, the Thibetan language is the only vehicle of communication; while in Assam, with its numerous tribes, each with its own language, a million and a half of people speak Assamese, which is supposed to be a dialect of Bengáli. Leaving the frontier tribes from the Indus to the Brahmapootra, India proper, with all its 'nations and kindreds and peoples and tongues,' lies before us with its three families of languages—Indo-Aryan, Dravidian, and Kolarian, and their numerous offshoots and subdivisions. Seven languages at least are grouped under the name of Kolarian, and of these the best known are the Santal, the Munda, the Ho, spoken by more than three millions. The Indo-Aryan vernaculars are spoken over a wider area and by a far larger number of people than any other Indian language, and they belong to the same family as our own and most of the other languages of Europe. In Lower Bengal, Bengáli is spoken by 36,000,000; Oriya by 5,000,000; Hindî, including its Mohammedan dialect of Urdû, is spoken by more than 100,000,000; Panjâbi by 12,000,000. Then in

Bombay Sindhî is spoken by 2,000,000 ; Gujerâthî by 7,000,000 ; Marâthî by 15,000,000. In consequence of the wide area over which these languages are spoken, and of the isolation in which, until recently, the people lived, a variety of dialects have sprung up, and it is said that of Hindî alone there are twelve distinct dialects. The Dravidian languages, twelve in number, not reckoning local dialects, are spoken in every part of Madras, in the southern portion of the Bombay presidency, in the Central Provinces, and even in some isolated parts of the presidency of Bengal. Not to do more than mention the Orâons, the Santhals, the Khônds of Orissa, the Gônds of the Central Provinces, the Tudas, and the Kotas, there stands out in prominence the Tamul, the most cultivated language of all, and possessing an extensive literature. It is spoken by 14,500,000; Telugu, the Italian of the East, is the language of 15,500,000 ; Canarese of 9,250,000 ; Malayâlim of 3,750,000. The people who speak the Dravidian languages are reckoned at 45,660,000.

Among these nations, differing so widely in race and tongue, there is one thing in common, a religious contempt for the English people as unclean, and a not unnatural jealousy of them as a conquering and usurping power. If the religions of India are fewer than its tongues, there is in them—at least in the foremost religions—a force of resistance to the Christian teacher which the religions of Greece and Rome could not oppose. These had no priestly caste, nor sacred books; but in Brahmanism, which is the faith of more than 187,000,000, we have a creed so ancient that its very origin is lost in

Antipathy to English as conquerors and rulers

the region of pre-historic myth, and a system which everywhere recognises the Divine, and prescribes, to an eminently conservative people, religious rites for every incident of life, from the cradle to the grave. Its sacred books date from at least 900 years before Christ, and that which we lightly speak of as *Caste*, and which some declare to be only a social institution, has welded together Hindu society, by the marvellous knowledge of human nature with which it is instinct, into a compact and wellnigh impregnable mass. So much is this system ingrained into the hearts of the people that the greatest sticklers for its unimpaired observance are the Sudras, who are the chief victims of its austerities. To receive baptism, to worship in a Christian church with an alien people, to receive the Holy Communion from an alien priest, is to place the Hindu convert at once and for ever outside the pale of humanity, and to separate him from every tie of family and kindred. Christianity has not been the only opponent of Brahmanism. In the seventh century before the Christian era, its supremacy was challenged, and the foremost of its reformers was Sakya Mouni, a king's son, in what is now the kingdom of Oudh; dissatisfied with the materialism and sacerdotalism of his religion, he gave himself up to meditation and asceticism. Neither the splendour of the Court nor the happiness of domestic life could divert him, and he devoted his life to the task of proclaiming the Divine light, which he believed to have entered into his own soul, whereby he became Buddha, the enlightened one. By his own labours, and by a system of missionary organisation which was adopted after his death, his creed covered Ceylon, Burmah, Siam, China, Tartary, and Thibet, and its presence was felt on the borders of European Russia. For a thousand years it was dominant in Hindostan, until a revival of Brahmanism expelled it. It absorbed into itself much of the Confucianism of China and Japan, and at this moment 450,000,000 profess this hopeless creed, which, in its dreamy apathy and childish superstition, is the most priest-ridden religion in the world. The third great religious system, Mohammedanism, is the only non-Christian creed which attempts the work of proselytism. Fifty millions of souls in India cling to it, and among them every class is to be found: the Sunni with his traditions, the Shiah with his laxer sentiment and his literary taste, the Pantheistic Sufi, the fanatical Wahábi, all of them feeling that their great argument—victory by the sword—has failed them, and that they must seek other means of conversion.

<small>Mohammedanism</small>

Against these three great systems the Church has sent forth scanty forces, badly equipped and meagrely supported. In each the wise missionary will discover some common ground. In Brahmanism, the last stronghold of antique paganism, which invests every hour and every relation of life with religious significance, the devout Christian sees something which is entitled to respect; for in the so-called materialism and sacerdotalism of this religion is an imperfect but striking analogy with the system of the Christian sacraments and priesthood, and in the system of Caste itself there is something which is closely connected with the doctrine of the Incarnation. The Hindu is familiar with the idea of an incarnation, is fully imbued with the

<small>Truths in common</small>

doctrine of an atonement, and his mind, while it will reject Christianity as an abstract system of philosophy, will more readily take in the conception of the brotherhood of the Christian Church. In Buddhism, effete and fossilised as it is, the attitude of its votaries is not disinclined to the attractions of the devotional Christian life; while in Mohammedanism, if only it were true to its own standards, we have in common the doctrine of the Fatherhood of God and the duty of temperance. But, while we admit with St. Augustine that 'every religion, however many its errors, has in it some real and divine truth,' we must not forget that the Hindu races are everywhere fossilised and powerless, that apathy and helplessness wrap themselves round the followers of Buddha, and that a moral blight uniformly follows in the train of Islam. The Koran and the Vedas contain gems of thought for which the world is the richer; but our admiration is checked when we know that such passages are only extracts from a mass of matter so foul and degrading that it has been found impossible to select continuous portions of sufficient length to set in the Government examinations which should not offend the most tolerant canons of taste.

So much for the systems against which it is our duty to lay siege. The difficulties which they present are enormous; there are other hindrances and difficulties, generally of a negative kind, on our own side. The men who conquered and governed India were the greatest soldiers and statesmen of their time; their country grudged them nothing; they had money, troops, advisers, colleagues at their desire. The men who have attempted the conversion of India have, with some notable exceptions, been men of only average ability, few in number, ill-supplied with worldly resources, often opposed, never supported by the civil power.

The same power has deprived the missionary Church of the exercise of its full liberties, and this probably is due to the lack of foresight on the part of the Church herself. When in 1814, on the representations of Wilberforce and others, a bishop and three archdeacons were accorded by Parliament to India, there was not a single clergyman of the English Church engaged in missionary work in the land. The whole clerical body consisted of the chaplains of the East India Company, which had been compelled to relax its opposition to missionary work generally. The bishop was but a chaplain-general in episcopal orders, and his position was one of limited authority, unique probably in the whole scope of ecclesiastical history. He was consecrated under letters patent from the Crown; but whereas the letters patent[1] issued on the consecration of a colonial bishop set forth that the nominee of the Crown, when duly consecrated, 'may by virtue of such appointment and consecration enter into and possess the said bishop's see as bishop thereof, without let or impediment from us, our heirs and successors, for the term of his natural life,' the nomination and appointment of the

Hindrances to Church growth in India

Limited episcopate

---

[1] The phrase runs: 'Such bishop shall not have or use any jurisdiction or exercise any episcopal functions whatsoever, either in the East Indies or elsewhere, but only such jurisdiction and functions as shall or may from time to time be limited to him by His Majesty by letters patent under the great seal of the United Kingdom.'

Bishop of Calcutta was declared to be 'subject to such power of revocation and recall as is by law vested in us and our successors.' This has been repeated in all subsequent letters patent; and the jurisdiction of the present metropolitan, as of his predecessors, is declared to be 'subject nevertheless to the general superintendence and revision of the Archbishop of Canterbury for the time being.' Thus, on the two occasions on which bishops have been consecrated in India, the consecration has taken place under a commission from the Archbishop of Canterbury, the Indian bishops being unable to consecrate *mero motu*.

In the course of years the whole condition of things has been changed, but the law remains the same. In 1814, the ecclesiastical establishment was coextensive with the whole clerical body; every year made this to be less and less the case. At present there is not an established Church in India; but there is within the Church an establishment, much limited and restricted by Acts of Parliament, which is a very serious hindrance to the growth of the whole Church. The clerical body in India now numbers about 625, of whom about 165, including the bishops, are chaplains. No priest is eligible for the office of archdeacon unless he be a chaplain. Of the remaining 460 about 68 are engaged in education, in ministering to Europeans on plantations, in harbours, and in smaller towns; and the remainder, the vast majority of the whole, are missionaries, and of these again 217 are natives of India. The existence of an ecclesiastical establishment for the benefit of the servants of the Crown who hold India in subjection and peace is as much to be

Changes demanded

justified as the maintenance of a medical staff, who shall care for the physical health of these classes; and it is quite just that these establishments should be maintained by the taxation of the land. But no injustice could be more patent than to tax a heathen people for the maintenance of a clergy who should attempt their conversion. Thus the bishops and chaplains are by their appointment, and still more by the Royal proclamation of 1858 precluded from any interference with the religious beliefs of the people.[1]

For the due prosecution of the work of the Church the bishops of India must be multiplied and their chief work must be evangelistic; for the English population will never increase as in a colony. If the establishment cannot become missionary, as no one desires that it should, the chaplains must be placed with their missionary brethren under their natural superiors in spiritual things, who need have no connection with the State. The present anomalous state of things is fatal to all growth. No statesman will bring Indian ecclesiastical matters before Parliament; and without Parliamentary action the repressive force of ancient Acts remains and forbids absolutely the erection of bishoprics within the

[1] The following is the passage referred to:—'Firmly relying ourselves on the truth of Christianity, and acknowledging with gratitude the solace of religion, we disclaim alike the right and the desire to impose our convictions on any of our subjects. We declare it to be our Royal will and pleasure that none be in anywise favoured, none molested or disquieted, by reason of their religious faith or observances, but that all shall alike enjoy the equal and impartial protection of the law; and we do strictly charge and enjoin those who may be in authority under us that they abstain from all interference with the religious belief or worship of any of our subjects, on pain of our highest displeasure.'

limits of the dominions of the East India Company in 1814 when the see of Calcutta was formed, or in any other part of India without the consent of the civil authorities; neither can a bishop hold any see in British India unless he accepts the obligations involved in the position and status of a chaplain. A bishop of the ordinary type, free from all civil restrictions, labours in the protected State of Travancore; but in Madras, where the large missions demand episcopal care always at hand, the exigencies of the position have driven the Church to the unsatisfactory arrangement whereby two veteran missionaries supervise the missions of two societies, not as bishops with independent authority but under a commission from the Bishop of Madras, revocable at any moment, and absolutely at an end on the vacancy of the see.

<small>Travancore</small>

<small>Tinnevelly</small>

The growth of the Church, whether among Europeans or among heathen tribes, is shown in other lands to be largely dependent on a vigorous episcopate increased freely as occasion demands: the stunted condition of a large portion of the Church in India justifies the belief that the root and cause of its stagnation is the impossibility of expanding its work and increasing its organisation with the freedom elsewhere enjoyed.

CHAPTER XIV.

MISSIONS IN THE EAST INDIES (*continued*).

WHEN Bishop Middleton was sent to Calcutta in 1814 he had everything to begin. There was scarcely a decent church, but Divine service was held in riding-schools, in verandahs, in any place where people could be sheltered. The chaplains of the Company did not desire his presence, and were content to regard the Governor-General as their ordinary. He was nevertheless bound hand and foot by precedents and legal restrictions. When he wished to ordain some of the catechists whom Schwartz had trained and who had been working for the Church, the Act of Uniformity immediately confronted him. He was told that he could perform service only in English, and that as the candidates were not British subjects they could not take the oath of supremacy, nor could it be dispensed with. Bishop Middleton never ordained a native of India; but he saw the necessity of founding a college in which the converts should be educated for the ministry, and in 1820 he laid the foundation of Bishop's College at Howrah on the opposite side of the Hooghley. This institution has now been transferred to Calcutta; but it must be admitted that the very little progress which missions have made in Bengal has shown that the college was and is in advance of the times, and that so far it has failed to realise the intentions of its founder. In 1817 the Government added to the charge

Bishop Middleton's position of difficulties 1814-1823

Bishop's College founded

of the Bishop of Calcutta the Island of Ceylon; in 1823 'all British subjects within the limits of the East India Company's charter and in islands north of the equator and all places between the Cape of Good Hope and Magellan's Straits,' and in 1824, 'New South Wales with its dependencies.'

In 1823 the poet-bishop Heber succeeded Middleton, and in 1826 he died at Trichinopoly, while ministering to the converts of Schwartz. After the two very brief episcopates of Bishops James and Turner, Bishop Daniel Wilson in 1832, at the age of fifty-four, commenced an episcopate which lasted until 1857. In 1835 he obtained the establishment, by Act of Parliament, of the see of Madras, and in 1837 of that of Bombay. In 1847 he consecrated the cathedral at Calcutta, to which he had contributed the munificent sum of 20,000*l*. He visited Penang and Burmah, where no Anglican bishop had ever set foot: against the system of caste he waged an unflinching war, while his personal piety and bold reproof of vice raised the whole tone of spiritual life in India. He died at a time of national fear and humiliation. His last sermon was preached on July 24, 1857, a day appointed by himself as a day of fasting. It was a dark hour: the Mutiny was raging through the land. Sir Henry Lawrence was dead: Delhi and Cawnpore and Lucknow were in the hands of a fanatical and mutinous soldiery: Calcutta might be the next position to be seized. But the good and brave old man prayed and consoled and cheered; at the same time he denounced the unchristian policy of the Government and the irreligious lives of too many of the English as having called down Divine vengeance.

The great statesman-bishop Cotton came to India at a critical time. The Mutiny was suppressed, but not the spirit which had prompted it; there was still much disaffection. Force had compelled subordination, but of loyalty there was no sign. The country had to be pacified; the missions to be re-established, in some cases to be rebuilt on ruins red with the blood of those who had been murdered. The bishop saw that gradually the English population had been receiving new elements; that railways and tea plantations and telegraphic works had brought to India hundreds of persons, wholly separate from the civil and military servants of the East India Company, or of the Crown which had now supplanted it. For these he founded the Additional Clergy Society, which provides the ministrations of the Church for the Europeans and Eurasians, who are under the care neither of Government chaplains nor of missionaries; and he established schools in the hills where in a cool climate the children of Anglo-Indians could be educated. By his accidental death, in October 1866, many plans of work which his fertile brain had set on foot were arrested.

Bishop Cotton, 1857-1866

His successor, Bishop Milman, was consecrated on February 2, 1867, and on March 25 was enthroned in his cathedral. The chief historical events of his episcopate were the reception into the communion of the Church of 7,000 Kôl Christians at Chota Nagpore, and of a large number of Karens at Tounghoo. These were events of great interest. When Bishop Cotton had completed his visitation tour over the whole

Bishop Milman, 1867-1876

province, he declared that there were three missionary successes in India—the work of the Church of England in Tinnevelly, of the Berlin Missionary Society in Chota Nagpore, and of the American Baptists in the Burmese mountains, and now from these two last missions thousands were seeking admission into the Church of England. The Lutheran missionaries had come to India in 1844, not having determined where they should commence their work, and in Calcutta they found some Kôls repairing the roads. Struck by their appearance, so different from that of the Bengalis, they inquired who they were, and finding that their race was settled in the central plateau, and was without any missionaries, they took up their abode at Ranchi. For five years they made not a single convert. Then four Kôls, who had read portions of a Hindi New Testament, came to the mission-house and requested that they might 'see Jesus.' The missionaries spoke to them of the ascended Lord; but the poor people were dissatisfied and went away in anger. After a week they returned and submitted to be taught, and after seventeen years the converts numbered 10,000. Meanwhile Germany failed to send adequate funds. New missionaries arrived and disagreed with the older men, who had done all the work of twenty-two years. The founder, Pastor Gossner, on his death-bed had expressed a wish that the mission should be adopted by the Church of England, and in 1869, four of the missionaries were ordained by Bishop Milman, who received at the same time 7,000 persons into church fellowship. The mission has gone on increasing, and in 1885, when the Bishop of Calcutta visited the various villages, he found more than 13,000

The Kôls

baptized persons, with fifteen of their brethren ordained to minister among them.

In the same year the Bishop of Rangoon visited the Karen mission at Tounghoo, and found 4,000 Christians belonging to tribes which, before the advent of the missionaries, were always at deadly feud. Here again are five native clergymen and a staff of native catechists supported by the offerings of the people.

Bishop Milman strongly insisted on the necessity of the subdivision of the diocese. He did not live to see it accomplished; but probably his death, which was caused by the incessant attempt to compass work beyond the capacity of a man possessing even his physical strength and active mind, did much to remove the objections which had previously stood in the way. In 1877 the dioceses of Lahore and Rangoon were founded. Large sums were raised in England for the endowment; Dioceses of Lahore and Rangoon but the Government would not consent to the appointment of bishops who were not also chaplains. To Lahore the learned and experienced missionary Dr. French was consecrated; to Rangoon the Rev. J. H. Titcomb, a leading clergyman of the diocese of Winchester, which had raised a large portion of the endowment.

In the diocese of Lahore the historic city of Delhi is the scene of one of the most important missions in India. Delhi and the Mutiny of 1857 In 1852 the station chaplain, the Rev. M. E. Jennings, moved a few members of his congregation to join with him in doing something for the 175,000 people whom they saw daily before them living in idolatry or in fanatical Mohammedanism. He knew that some of them were seeking the truth. In that same year Mr. Jennings baptized two native gentlemen of high position, one the station surgeon, Chimmum Lall, the other Lala Ram Chandra, a man of great mathematical attainments, a professor in the Presidency College. The Propagation Society took up the mission, and gave 8,000*l*. towards the cost of its establishment. Two clergymen were sent out, who opened a good school and gathered together a little congregation; then, without a word of warning, the Mutiny broke out over the whole of the N.W. Provinces. At Agra and Lahore the English and the native Christians found shelter within the walls; at Cawnpore two missionaries of the Propagation Society were murdered; the Rev. A. Macallum was killed at Shahjehanpore; four American Presbyterian missionaries and their families perished at Futteyghur; two members of the same mission were killed at Sealkote; while at Delhi the mission was extinguished. The chaplain and his daughter, and an officer who had warmly supported the mission, were among the first victims. The Rev. A. Hubbard, two catechists, and Chimmum Lall were seized and offered life and liberty if they would renounce their Christianity; but they wavered not, and at once the crown of martyrdom was won. A catechist and three ladies belonging to the Baptist mission in Delhi bore the same noble testimony and shared the same fate.

Before the Mutiny was quite stamped out volunteers were on their way to Delhi. The Rev. T. Skelton, Fellow of Queen's College, Cambridge, refounded the Society's mission in 1859, and here he was greeted by Ram Chandra, who continued until his death, in 1883, to be the staunch supporter of the Church, while his blameless and devout manner of life was a gospel daily preached to the heathen. Memorial churches were built both at Delhi and Cawnpore, and the Church Missionary Society built another at the great city of Amritzar.

In 1877 a movement within the University of Cambridge led to some members of that University undertaking missionary work in India, and they were advised by Sir Bartle Frere to connect themselves and their work with the Delhi mission of the Propagation Society, where the Rev. R. R. Winter with several colleagues had been labouring with much wisdom for many years. It was felt that a body of University men living together might devote themselves with much advantage to the work of higher education. Experience has shown that it is needful to work on a broader basis, and the accession of a body of graduates, generally five in number, has given to the Delhi staff a contingent such as ought to be found in every large city in India. From Delhi as a centre the mission extends over a large tract of country, stations being established as far as seventy miles away.

The Delhi mission reinforced by Cambridge

In the northern parts of India the Church Missionary Society has a large organisation covering the land, and reaching to Cashmere. During the Mutiny the British rule in the North was saved by the Punjab. The gallant soldiers and administrators who ruled it and restored the British supremacy over the land, the two Lawrences, Edwardes, Macleod, Montgomery, and their colleagues, broke through the traditions of the service, and boldly

Missions of Church Missionary Society in North India

proclaimed their ardent faith as Christians. 'We may be quite sure,' said Sir Herbert Edwardes, 'that we are much safer if we do our duty than if we neglect it, and that He who has brought us here with His own right arm will shield and bless us if, in simple reliance upon Him, we try to do His will.'

In Bombay, mission work is not so advanced as in some other parts of India; less has been attempted and smaller expenditure has been incurred. Until the arrival of Bishop Douglas in 1869 the missionaries were chiefly stationed in or near the city of Bombay. Now a chain of stations far apart from each other has been formed. Little or no impression has been made on the Parsis or on the higher classes, but in the Ahmednagur district the conversion of the Mahars, a low caste race, has been very remarkable, and it is said that, given an adequate staff, the whole race would in a short time be evangelised.

Bombay

In Rangoon, where the prevalent religion is Buddhism, and where consequently caste does not oppose itself, the work of the Church is full of encouragement. Education, for which the people are eager, has ever been a prominent feature. From St. John's College in Rangoon, the headmaster and some of his pupils were invited to Mandalay by the king in 1868, with the result that the king built a church, school, and clergy-house at his own cost, allowing no one to share in the honour except Her Majesty, who gave a marble font. The king died in 1878 and was succeeded by the notorious Theebaw, whose conduct led to the withdrawal of all English Residents in the following year. On January 1, 1886,

Rangoon

Upper Burma was added to the British Empire, and Theebaw was deposed. The Mission was reopened, and with the changed condition of things the prospects of the country are brightened. The people will live under just laws, and the land will be able to develop its treasures. The Irrawaddy was the high road to China until the Mohammedan outbreak in Yunnan in 1853-4, and the annexation of this country will probably re-open a way to China and to Thibet, where, beyond a station of the Moravians and a mission of the Russian Church in the far North, Christianity is not represented.

<small>Opening of Upper Burma</small>

In the city of Rangoon, St. John's College is sending out a continual supply of well-educated Burmans, who are holding good positions all over the country, and a Native Training College will supply a Burmese Ministry at an early day. The successful mission to the Karens has already been alluded to.

Ceylon, although belonging to the province of Calcutta, is for civil purposes an English colony. Its ecclesiastical history is peculiar. When the Dutch were driven out of the island in 1795, they left 350,000 Protestant Christians behind them. In 1811, when the island came under British rule, these had dwindled to 150,000. The Portuguese were believed to have left a body of converts hardly inferior in number to those of the Dutch. When Bishop Chapman arrived in 1846 he found the English clergy and the churches insufficient in number, and many heathen ceremonies, as well as others peculiar to the Church of Rome, incorporated in the worship of the Church. The good bishop founded St. Thomas's College, and in 1854

<small>Ceylon</small>

consecrated the cathedral church of Colombo. The northern half of the island is peopled chiefly with Hindus akin to the Shanars in Tinnevelly and speaking Tamil; there are also some immigrants from Malabar, and in the interior of the island some aboriginal tribes still linger in unredeemed savagery. In the southern portion the people are generally Singhalese by race and Buddhists by religion. Concurrent endowment of religious bodies has prevailed in Ceylon; but the Imperial Parliament has given notice that after five years from 1881 no fresh obligations will be incurred by Government, and attempts are now being made to secure for the bishopric and for the clergy independent endowments.

It is in Southern India that Christian missions have had their most marked success. It was here that the East India Company established their first settlement; but for sixty years there was no church nor other outward sign of the Englishman's religion. The Church of Rome early occupied the field, and the Jesuit Fathers from their central home at Madura extended their missions over a very wide area, under the direction of the authorities at Goa. Ziegenbalg, as has been already mentioned, founded the Tranquebar mission in 1705. In 1726 the Christian Knowledge Society supported the missions, but the labourers were all Lutherans. Schwartz and Kohlhoff and their brethren won the respect of all; and on the death of Schwartz in 1798 the Rajah of Tanjore, himself a heathen, raised a monument to his memory. In 1787 there were 17,000 Christians in the district of Tranquebar alone; but the work was the work of single souls without

South India

unity and without cohesion; and when the Propagation Society took over the twelve missions of the older society in 1824, there were only five missionaries, and of these only three were resident at their stations. In 1814 the Church Missionary Society commenced a magnificent and far-reaching work in Southern India; and the two societies have by their educational and evangelistic agencies changed the face of the country. It must also be stated that the Wesleyan and London Missionary Societies, the Presbyterians, both Free and Established, the German and American societies, have also occupied the land with happy results.

The Government census describes the people of Southern India as Hindu in religion. This is true in that Brahmanism prevails in the towns, and the Hindu deities are worshipped by the higher classes; but the religion of the masses is practically devil-worship. They live under the perpetual bondage of fear, and their religious observances consist of sacrifices which may avert the wrath of malignant deities. The following account is from the pen of Bishop Caldwell:—'The devils worshipped by the people in their heathen state, unlike the indolent deities of Brahminical mythology, are supposed to be ever "going to and fro in the earth, and wandering up and down in it," seeking for opportunities of inflicting evil. In every undertaking, in all the changes of life and in every season and place, the anger of devils is believed to be impending. Every bodily ailment which does not immediately yield to medicine is supposed to be a possession of the devil. The fever produced by the bite of a rat is found difficult to cure, and the native doctor

Devil-worship

tells the name of the five devils that resist the force of his art. An infant cries all night, and a devil is said to be in it. An ill-built house falls down, and a devil receives the blame. Bullocks take fright at night, and a devil is said to have scared them. These instances, which are only a specimen of what constantly occurs, will serve to show how the people are all their life subject to the bondage of superstitious fear. In this neighbourhood in particular, in which denser ignorance than I have ever elsewhere met with in Tinnevelly has always prevailed, the heathen are wholly given up to superstition. I know a hamlet containing only nine houses, where thirteen devils are worshipped. This fear of the anger of demons acts in two ways prejudicially. It deters many from placing themselves under Christian instruction, and drives away many before they have acquired the first principles of knowledge and faith. It also often lies dormant in the minds of even the better-instructed and more advanced converts, sifting and sapping their confidence in God, and sometimes, during the prevalence of cholera, or under the pressure of calamity (especially when they think their children dangerously ill), tempting them to make shipwreck of their faith.'

Self-help in the native Church A people born and living in these surroundings have shown, nevertheless, a great capacity for spiritual enlightenment, and a great zeal in communicating to their brethren the privileges which they have themselves received. From the first they have been trained in this duty. Village after village has been brought under Christian teaching by the efforts of their neighbours, themselves, in the majority of cases perhaps, unable to read. Self-help has also from the first been a characteristic of the South Indian Church. Although the converts are the poorest of the poor, they have from the first paid for their religion, and so have learned to value it. In no part of the world has the native ministry been so marked a feature of the work, and from the first the native clergy have not been wholly dependent on funds from England.

In 1873 the Church in Tinnevelly had grown to a position which made it absolutely necessary that a *Bishops in Tinnevelly* bishop should be resident in the midst of it; but it was not until 1877 that two veteran missionaries, Dr. Caldwell and Dr. Sargent, were consecrated in Calcutta, under a commission from the Archbishop of Canterbury, coadjutor bishops to the Bishop of Madras. In that same year first floods and then famine desolated Tinnevelly. Large sums of money were given by Government, and munificent offerings were sent from England for the relief of the starving multitudes. It was a remarkable testimony to the value of the missionaries living among the people, that the Government was largely dependent on their experience for the distribution of the food which had been purchased. The people were ready to be moved by any outward exhibition of the power of Christianity. The missionaries had for years been exercising over *The famine and its teaching* them an influence of which they were themselves hardly conscious; and now the beneficence of Christians, living thousands of miles away, contrasted favourably with the indifference of Hinduism, from whose temples not a single anna had come for the relief of the starving, so that the people recognised the superiority of a religion of love over a religion of selfish indulgence. Therefore it was no wonder that between 30,000 and 40,000 people came and voluntarily placed themselves under Christian instruction. Their motives were mixed, no doubt; their action arose from no profound theological convictions, and they were very ignorant. But, whatever their motives, gratitude for past kindness rather than the expectation of it in the future must have been dominant; for it was not until the presence of famine was over that they sought spiritual food. The strain on the staff of missionaries which so large accessions caused was very great; but the large body of native catechists furnished deacons in good number, and the missionary clergy in the diocese of Madras now number 163, of whom 136 are natives, supported in almost every instance partially or entirely by their native congregations.

It cannot be said that missions which have attained to this point of development are failures. True, Southern India is the bright example; but all over the great peninsula results, positive or negative, are capable of being registered. The older systems of Indian religions are being undermined; the introduction of railways and other products of Western civilisation is the knell of Brahmanism and Buddhism; the writings of sceptics, for which Orientals have an eager appreciation, will destroy their ancestral faiths without substituting another. The very existence of the Brahmo Somaj forebodes the doom of Hinduism; but whether its followers will go beyond the theism which at present seems to content them, who can tell? There are many disintegrating influences at work which cannot be accurately appraised, but time will show what they are accomplishing. Meanwhile graduates of Indian universities are now working in the missions, and students of our Indian theological colleges distinguish themselves in the Oxford and Cambridge Preliminary Theological Examinations. The proportion of Christians to non-Christians in India is still painfully small. According to the census of 1881, out of every 10,000 of the population of India 73 only are Christians; but the impartial opinion of the writer of the census-report volunteers the statement that 'a few years will show a very large accession to the numbers of the various Christian churches. The closest observers are almost unanimous in the opinion that the ground has already been cleared for such a movement; but their views are not so much in accord as to the class from which the accession will be made.' The rate of increase of the Christian population in the province of Madras in the ten years 1871–81 was 30·39 per cent.

Proportion of Christians to non-Christians

In the presence of a work so gigantic, however much the divisions of Christianity are to be deplored, it is thankworthy that all Christian bodies recognise the claims of India, and that their representatives in their work abroad refrain from mutual proselytism, and think more of points of agreement than of difference. It is obvious, too, that in so wide and varied a field there is abundant scope for the free exercise of all gifts and every kind of missionary machinery.

Need of all kinds of work

So long as the women of India are immured in gloomy zenanas and harems, the work of elevating and converting the mothers of the next generation must be entrusted to their white sisters;

Woman's work in India

and women's work as teachers, as doctors, as nurses, must be placed in a position second only to that of the ordained evangelist. There is scope for the work of education; and no teaching can rightly be depreciated as secular, if it be given by one who is himself a Christian. There is need of the preacher who will go into the streets and bazaars and proclaim the Gospel, and be ready, with gravity and sympathy, to argue with the Mahometan or Hindu pundit. There is a boundless field for the exercise of the art of healing; and medical missionaries of both sexes, and trained Christian nurses are likely to contribute much more to the work in the future than they have in the past. The married missionary has it in charge to set forth before the heathen the domestic side of Christianity, and a pattern of family life; and many a missionary's wife has done for the work of the Divine Master what no priest could have done. There is ample room for the man who, denying himself the happiness of domestic life, will show what is the Christian conception of the asceticism with which their own fakeers and monks have made Orientals familiar. Unfortunately it has not always been remembered that there is no one royal method of work, and that all the various methods are but parts of a system of which each element will contribute, under God's favour, to the common consummation. The man who values one method is tempted sometimes to depreciate all others, and indeed the introduction of almost every new method has been marked by a depreciation of all that have gone before, in entire forgetfulness of the fact that earlier labours have made subsequent ventures possible.

Medical missions, education, bazaar-preaching

Domestic life and asceticism

CHAPTER XV.

MISSIONS IN CHINA, JAPAN, AND BORNEO.

WHATEVER the difficulties presented by the India of to-day, they are not to be compared with those which confront the Church in China. The land is still a land of mystery, treaties and open ports notwithstanding. We know so little of it that the number of the population has been placed by some as low as 150,000,000, by others as high as 400,000,000. Then the languages! for the dialects of one part of the empire are utterly unknown in others; and nowhere is there a phonetic alphabet, but each character represents a separate word, with distinct sound and meaning. Then the people! conservative beyond conception, proud of their ancient civilisation, which forty centuries ago was hardly behind its present condition, and despising all foreigners as barbarians. Then the religions! Confucianism, with its Pantheism and Emperor-worship; Taōism, with its apathy, which condemns the exercise of judgment and intelligence; and Buddhism in its most corrupt form.

Roman Catholic missions in China. The Church of Rome entered on the task of converting China in the thirteenth century, and its converts at this day are four times the number of the aggregate of those of all other religious bodies. In the seventeenth century the Jesuits, after seeming to hold China in their grasp, were driven from the country, and the native hatred of foreigners and their creed was intensified, but they left their mark behind them in a body of believers whom persecution could not terrify. Early in the present century the London Missionary Society sent a missionary to China, and to him the world is indebted for the first good translation of the Scriptures into Chinese. To another agent of that society we owe a translation of the religious classics of the empire. Successive treaties, dating from the war in 1842, have in course of time so far opened the land as to give to Europeans the right of residence at twenty great centres, and Christianity is now free to make its way without reasonable fear of interruption. In 1844 the American Church sent a mission with a bishop at its head to Shanghae. Bishop Boone, who combined with other gifts a knowledge of medicine, laboured in China for twenty years, and was followed in 1866 by Bishop Williams, who subsequently limited his work to Japan; and a remarkable man, Bishop Schereschewsky, who succeeded him, translated the whole Bible and Prayer-Book into the Mandarin tongue. The Church Missionary Society commenced a mission as soon as the ports were open. In 1849 the first English bishop was consecrated and had his cathedral and college at Hong-Kong. In 1872 another bishopric was planted at Ningpo, and in 1880 another bishop was entrusted with the charge of North China, where the S. P. G. had commenced missionary work in 1874. While the adherents of the Church of Rome are estimated at 600,000, it is believed that the Christians of other bodies number 150,000, and that 200 foreign mis-

Marginalia: The London Missionary Society. The American Church in China. The C. M. S. Mission. The Episcopate. The S. P. G. Mission.

sionaries, and about 500 natives, in the character of preachers, evangelists, and teachers, are labouring for the people's conversion. The China Inland Mission, which professes to be undenominational, has sent a number of evangelists, two and two, into every province of the empire. They adopt Chinese dress, and have won much respect wherever they have gone. It is open to question whether a purely itinerating mission, without permanent head-quarters, is likely to effect abiding results; but the field is so vast that every experiment claims sympathy. It has already been suggested that the greatest blow to Chinese paganism may be dealt by its own children who have been converted in other lands. Their enterprising spirit carries the Chinese into all parts of the world where cheap labour is desired. Removed from his native land the Chinaman saves money, which he has no inducement to do at home, for if reputed to be a capitalist he would soon be 'squeezed' by the mandarins. He is also ready to listen to the Christian teacher when separated from the traditions and prejudices of his home, and when converted is a staunch and self-denying Christian. The Chinese converts build their own churches and try to bring others to the faith, and on their return to China generally remain true to their new faith, and in many instances strive zealously to propagate it. Abyssinia was converted in the fourth century by two youths, who having been taken captive, and in the land of their captivity been brought to Christ, went home and made their country to share in what they had themselves been taught by strangers. May the story be repeated in China!

China Inland Mission

Chinese converts in other lands

In Japan, as in China, the credit of being the first in the field is due to the Church of Rome. In 1549 St. Francis Xavier commenced his crusade. He spent but two years in the country, but he commenced a magnificent work, and in less than forty years Romanism gained such ascendency that a Japanese embassy was sent to Pope Gregory XIII. with letters and valuable gifts. But the rulers gradually realised the fact that if Christianity prevailed, their own authority would disappear, and in 1587 the first edict for the expulsion of missionaries was passed. Still, Christianity had its adherents among the nobles, and it was found that the edict could not be put in force without civil war. The dominant party subjected the Christians to persecution and tortures; and in 1637, 30,000 Christians, who had suffered for the faith, were buried in one grave, over which was written, 'So long as the sun shall warm the earth, let no Christian be so bold as to come to Japan.' The profession of Christianity was a capital offence. The symbol of the cross was with much ceremony publicly trampled on once every year. So recently as the beginning of this century some persons were crucified at Osaka for 'superstition,' probably another name for Christianity; and the boards which were erected in the seventeenth century at cross-roads and bridges with the proclamation, 'The evil sect called Christians is strictly forbidden; informers will be rewarded,' were not removed until 1869.

Thus the land remained absolutely closed until 1854, when the United States made a treaty which, very limited in its terms, broke through the isolation in which

the empire had been wrapped for two centuries. In 1858 Lord Elgin made a treaty which opened six important places to trade, and allowed a diplo-
matic agent to reside at Yeddo, the capital.
The Americans and the Romanists immediately entered, and the question arose, 'Was there any vestige of Christianity which had survived two centuries of persecution?' At first no sign appeared; but on looking closer, it was found that a large number of persons had surreptitiously maintained, as a kind of freemasonry, a profession of Christianity, and had secretly baptized their children, but with a formula so mutilated as to forbid the belief that the faith had been retained with any intelligent grasp of its meaning.

The country opened by treaty

Latency of Christianity

Unlike the Chinese, the people of Japan have shown an eagerness to listen to Christianity and a readiness to embrace it which suggests fears for their perseverance. The accessions became so numerous that it was found to be necessary that each of the Church missions should have its own bishop, as the oversight which could be
given to the English missions by a bishop
resident in China proved to be very insufficient. The resolutions of the Lambeth Conference of 1878 amply provided for the contingency of two bishops of sister churches being placed in the same country; and with due regard to the covenants thus made, the Rev. A. W. Poole was consecrated as bishop of the English Church in Japan in 1883, but died within two years. Two converts of the American Church were ordained in the same year, and in 1884 the first deacon of the English Mission, Yamagata Youegai, was ordained at Tokio, his congregation taking great interest in the

Japanese converts

service, and pledging themselves to provide a maintenance for him. Events have moved in Japan with a rapidity that may well give rise to fear. Bishop Bickersteth succeeds to a state of things wholly changed since the death of his predecessor. The eagerness of all classes to study English has led to its being made compulsory in the Government schools, and has opened all schools to the missionaries who are free to teach Christianity; the use of the Roman character is rapidly displacing the old and difficult Japanese characters, and in matters of social intercourse foreign etiquette is being substituted for the almost sacred ceremonial which has been the rule in Japan. A still greater change was recently made, distinctly as a concession to Christianity; Buddhism ceased to be the state religion, and the obligation to register a change of faith, which subjected the converts to much persecution, was abrogated.

From Japan the mission must make its way to the Corea, which, with its population of thirteen millions, is now partially open to the world. The late Sir Harry Parkes concluded a treaty with the Coreans, a fierce people under a weak government, in which he managed to insert a clause that British subjects should have full liberty for the exercise of their religion. More than that he could not obtain; but it is about as much as Lord Elgin obtained in his treaty with Japan; and whatever its value, it has led a body of American Presbyterians to enter the country.

The Corea

The mission to Borneo naturally groups itself with the story of China and Japan. In the sixteenth century Borneo, or Bruni, was the name of a city, the capital of a kingdom, which, from the number

Borneo

of Chinese who had settled there for the purposes of trade, might have been called a Chinese kingdom. There were at that time 25,000 houses in Bruni, but its trade left it, and the several ports had become only refuges for pirates who swept the Chinese seas. In 1830 an English gentleman cruising in his own yacht was struck by the beauty of the islands, which were lying neglected. He formed a scheme for suppressing piracy, extirpating slavery, and opening the island to trade. In 1838 he returned with a suitable yacht and well-drilled crew, and having helped the native rajah to put down a rebellion, he was offered the province of Sarâwak. In 1841 he was proclaimed rajah, his authority being confirmed by the Sultan of Borneo. In answer to the appeal of Rajah Brooke, two clergymen went to Borneo in 1848, of whom one, the Rev. F. T. M'Dougall, was in 1855 consecrated Bishop of Labuan. Mr. M'Dougall was a medical man, and his skill was soon put into operation, a dispensary, which grew into a hospital, being at once opened. Other missionaries joined Mr. M'Dougall, who in the meantime had acquired Malay and Chinese, had translated much, and had made visits of inquiry into the interior, that he might know where to place men as they came out. From time to time, when the missions were hopefully growing, outbreaks occurred, which for a time put a stop to everything. In 1857 the Chinese attacked the English, killing some of the rajah's officers and driving the bishop with his family and the converts into the jungle. This roused the passions of the Dyaks, who, under the influence of the missionaries, had adopted a peaceful

Rajah Brooke

Bishop M'Dougall

mode of life. Their old love of head-taking was nevertheless strong, and it was long before they again settled down. In 1859 a Mohammedan plot was hatched and two Englishmen were killed. Prospects brightened when in 1863 a notorious pirate, having met with some Christian Dyaks, voluntarily placed himself under instruction. The next year he brought his wife and child, and then returned to persuade the people of his tribe. In 1867 a missionary visited this people, who had been notorious for piracy and head-taking, and baptized 180 persons. Of the various tribes of Dyaks, living on several rivers and speaking different dialects, at least 3,000 are now members of the English Church. No attempt has been made to compel the Dyaks who have embraced Christianity to give up any customs which are not inconsistent with decency and morality. In laying the foundations of a church in Borneo, it has been recognised from the first that the race is in its own land, that there are no signs of its having emigrated from any other part of the world, and that it is likely to increase both in numbers and in importance.

Much attention has been given to the Chinese in Borneo. In 1849, 3,000 of them arrived in the island, and one of their number was among the first inquirers into Christianity, and after a long probation as catechist he was ordained deacon. The Chinese here, as in other lands, have shown great religious sincerity. Of themselves they conceived the idea of building 'a house of charity' in Sarâwak for the shelter of fellow-Christians in want, and for the reception of their countrymen dwelling up the rivers when business called them to the capital. The offertories

Chinese in Borneo

at their services enabled them to carry out the design, and the 'house of charity' has its place among the institutions of the diocese.

Within the last seven years a Company, which has received a Royal Charter of a fashion which recalls the early days of the East India Company, has occupied a large tract of country in Northern Borneo, rich in minerals and possessing moreover a fertile soil. At present, beyond a small number of Englishmen, the servants of the Company are Chinese, and for them provision was at once made by the Church.

<small>North Borneo Company</small>

In 1869 the Straits Settlements were removed from the diocese of Calcutta and placed under the charge of the Bishop of Labuan, who now takes the double title of Singapore and Saráwak. Singapore is a meeting-place of nations, and up and down the straits not fewer than 300,000 Mohammedans are scattered. At Singapore services are held in Tamil, Chinese, Singhalese, and Malay.

<small>Singapore</small>

The foresight of Sir Stamford Raffles recognised the value of this place, and from a fishing village of 150 souls it has grown to an important town with a population of 140,000, of whom more than one-half are Chinese. The same wise governor built a church, which is now replaced by a more ambitious structure, known as the cathedral church of St. Andrew, and endowed an educational institution, of which he wrote, 'I trust in God that this building may be the means of civilising and bettering the condition of millions.' At the several colonies in the Straits—Malacca, Perak, Penang, and Province Wellesley—provision is made for the spiritual care of the English settlers, and each church is made the centre of some evangelistic work among Chinese, Tamils, or Malays.

CHAPTER XVI.

CONCLUSION.

THE survey that we have taken of the progress of missionary work would be incomplete without some further consideration of the means by which it has been accomplished. The material means have been in the first instance supplied by the mother country. The liberality of English churchmen has been organised by societies, whose labours have afforded scope for financial and administrative work of the highest order. These societies have always urged the need of centralised activity to carry on the work as a whole, on a broad view of the needs and opportunities that from time to time presented themselves. But though missionary enterprise must originate in England, the object has always been to foster self-supporting Christian communities in connection with their mother church.

Retrospect

From the beginning, whether the Church accompanies her emigrant children with the ministrations to which they have been accustomed from their baptism, or whether she sends the heralds of the Gospel to proclaim the truth to the heathen—to prevent the newly-planted Church from being for all time an exotic, it is necessary that every Christian should be compelled to take his share in the maintenance of the Church of which he is a member, and that he should contemplate, as within reasonable distance, the time when the Church will have taken root in the land, and will depend wholly on the charities of its own children for its continuance. Whether it be the weekly penny to which the negro congregations in the West Indies willingly pledge their members, or the contributions of rice or grain which the converts in India are trained to bring and pour out on the floor of the chancel every Sunday; or whether it be the assessment levied by the finance board of a colonial diocese on each parish, and then by the vestry of the parish on every member according to his ability, the principle is everywhere the same, and is everywhere the only true way of developing self-respect and independent growth, and of suppressing the selfish spirit inherent in our nature, which prompts to the indignity of mendicancy. It is profitable to those who are compelled to adopt it; and it is only just to those at home, whose contributions to foreign missions, coming, as the bulk of such gifts do come, from poor people, represent real self-denial, and demand a rigidly economical disbursement. It will be seen that the funds annually raised in Great Britain, large in their absolute amount, are very limited in comparison with the work which is already carried on, and with other work which has to be begun over a field nearly conterminous with the world itself. If new enterprises are to be commenced, older fields must as soon as possible be left to their own resources. The following table shows the amount raised, in the

Principles of financial administration

year 1884, for missionary purposes in Great Britain. It excludes all dividends and interest on investments, and gives simply the amounts of the annual contributions. The gross total was 1,216,530*l*., and is thus distributed :—

Church Societies	£491,647
Joint Societies of Churchmen and Nonconformists, such as the Bible Society, the Moravian Missions, &c.	182,085
English and Welsh Nonconformist Societies	391,046
Scotch and Irish Presbyterian Societies	193,208
Roman Catholic Societies	8,544

Endowments

These figures can of course give no guide to the result of past expenditure, which is seen in the endowments of colonial churches, or to the local contributions which are annually raised abroad. Thus nearly every colonial bishopric is endowed with an annual income ranging from 400*l*. to 2,000*l*. per annum, the exceptions being the few still dependent on grants from public funds, as in India, and some purely missionary dioceses, as in such countries as Madagascar and Japan, which are maintained by Societies. In many colonial dioceses there are General Clergy Endowment Funds, and not a few parishes with their own special endowments. The cathedrals are also more or less furnished with endowments, the gifts of colonial churchmen, which provide not merely for the maintenance of services, but for the theological teaching of the candidates for ordination. The various universities and colleges, which exist, sometimes in needless profusion, in our colonies, are a testimony to the liberality of the colonial laity ;

for, although probably in all cases the mother country has contributed liberally, the institutions would never have existed but for local gifts and local confidence in their administration. In North America, King's College at Windsor, Trinity College at Toronto, and Bishop's College at Quebec, are Church Universities, educating and giving degrees in each faculty, and planting out their students all over the Dominion. There is also a Theological College in Newfoundland, another in the far North-West at Prince Albert, and at Winnipeg St. John's College, in connection with the University of Manitoba, is provided with professorships, the holders of which constitute the cathedral staff. In the West Indies, Codrington College, affiliated with the University of Durham, gives a high education, under the influence of distinctly Church teaching. In Australia the Universities are holding up a high standard of secular education, and the Church is taking advantage of the curriculum while training her children in colleges affiliated. In India the various Theological Colleges, both of the Church and of dissenting communions, are training converts for the work of the ministry; and the High Schools and Mission Colleges send their pupils to the Universities with at least the amount of Christian influence which years of teaching at the hands of Christians may be supposed to impart. The independence of the mother country is perhaps more evident among colonial Dissenters than in the system of the Church. The Wesleyans in Australia and Canada, for example, have reproduced the Conference which in England is their supreme body, and are entirely self-governed.

Universities and Colleges

The next question to be considered is, how are these missions and colonial churches supplied with living agents? The foregoing pages have shown that in the colonies there exists a large store of institutions which can train an indigenous clergy, who from their surroundings, their family connections, and their own habits, are better calculated to serve the Church with advantage than men of similar gifts if sent from England. A few men of wider cultivation and larger experience, annually drafted into the colonial dioceses, will make their mark, to the great benefit of the Church; but they must be men of distinctly high gifts, or there is no need for them to leave their native country, and the need, such as it is, will become less and less as the several colonies develop, and colonial parents regard the priesthood as a natural and honourable profession for their sons. The Church has a right to look to the great Universities for men who shall build up the colonial churches and convert the heathen; but the supply of men from Oxford and Cambridge is probably less now than it was fifty years ago. Missions, which have about them some romance and adventure attract a few young graduates, who will spend four or five years abroad and then return to England, having added to the uncertainty which does so much harm to the progress of a mission; but for the long and slow work of acquiring an Oriental language and filling a place in the machinery of a mission whose success must come but slowly, the offers are very few. Hence the Church is driven to the colleges which specially train for foreign work, giving of necessity an education less wide and liberal than the old Universities. The Church Mis-

Supply of clergy

sionary Society established its college at Islington in 1825, and between 400 and 500 men have gone forth from its gates to foreign lands. In 1848 the ancient abbey of St. Augustine at Canterbury, after long desecration, was purchased and restored for the purpose of a missionary college. Since its opening, under the wardenship of Bishop Coleridge, the first bishop of Barbados, it has sent out nearly 300 students, of whom two have been raised to the episcopate, the Right Rev. Dr. Strachan, of Rangoon, and the Right Rev. Bransby Key, of St. John's, Kaffraria.

But given clergy, and means of their support, and a laity to whom they shall minister, where is the Organisation and administration machinery which shall govern and direct the whole body? The founders of the colonial churches do not appear to have thought of this. They were content to aim at reproducing as far as possible a counter-part of the Established Church to which they were accustomed at home. In North America the influence of the State distinctly aimed at this in the supposed interests of loyalty. Even the founders of the Colonial Bishoprics Council in 1841 seem to have been content if they obtained from the Crown letters patent constituting a see, and appropriating from public taxation an annual episcopal income. The letters patent were believed to convey coercive jurisdiction to the bishop who held them, and nothing more was desired. As dioceses multiplied and the necessity of forming provinces was recognised, again letters patent were invoked; and in 1847 Bishop Broughton became Metropolitan of Australia, and six years later Bishop Gray was made Metropolitan of South Africa. At the very first test the whole system broke down; and it was declared on the highest legal authority that the Crown had no power to grant coercive jurisdiction in a colony which had an independent legislature. It was obvious, therefore, that there was nothing to be done but to organise the various churches on the basis of voluntary consensual compact, which was, to quote the words of Mr. Gladstone in 1849, 'the basis on which the Church of Christ rested from the first.' The only alternative was a system of purely episcopal autocracy, under which no man of high standing or ability would consent to work. The colonial churches looked to England in vain; no help could come from thence, for Convocation had been silent for more than a century, and it was clear that synodal action in some form or other was essential. The very name frightened people, who saw in it a device for giving more power to the bishops. But, strange to say, the first bishop who attempted the task of holding a synod did it for the relief of himself. He wrote, ' I believe the monarchical idea of the episcopate to be as foreign to the true mind of the Church as it is adverse to the Gospel doctrine of humility.' This was Bishop Selwyn, who in 1844 held a synod of clergy; and in 1847 a second synod received from him a draft constitution which was the result of much consultation with high authorities in England. In 1850 the Australasian bishops met at Sydney, and laid down rules for the government of future synods, diocesan and provincial. The North American bishops formed themselves into a province, and the Crown made Montreal a metropolitical see in 1862, a distinction which

Failure of letters patent

Synodal action essential

Adopted in New Zealand, Australia, Canada,

it was soon shown the Crown had no power to confer. In 1857, Bishop Gray held his first synod at the Cape; and in about sixteen years from the date of the first provincial assemblage at Sydney, all the dioceses that were not in Crown colonies worked out for themselves a synodal system of government. Disestablishment has since given to the West Indian dioceses a like liberty, of which they have availed themselves.

<small>Africa, and West Indies</small>

To the bishops assembled at Sydney in 1850 is due the credit of recognising the right of the laity to a share in the legislation of the Church. True it is that on this occasion their share was limited to consultation and decision with the clergy of all matters affecting the temporalities of the Church; but, as a matter of history, it must be recorded that in every part of the world the equality of the three houses of bishops, clergy, and laity has been fully recognised, and the assent of all is essential to the passing of any statute or canon. Nor has there been any interference on the part of the laity with the legitimate freedom of the clergy; rather has it been the case that the lay House has proved itself the most conservative element of the synods. While the system of synodal government is in its broad principles everywhere the same, there are minor differences of detail which characterise the legislation of each province. Everywhere the synods are fully representative. The diocesan synods meet generally once in each year, under the presidency of the bishop. Every licensed priest has a seat, and every parish sends one representative communicant layman, elected by the whole body of his brother parishioners

<small>The laity in synod</small>

CONCLUSION

who declare themselves to be members of the Church. The provincial synods meet at longer intervals, generally triennially, as is the rule of the Convention of the Church of America. They consist of the bishops of the province, and elected clergy and laity, generally in equal numbers, from each diocese; and a quorum of one-third, in some cases of one-fourth, must be present. The bishops sit in a separate House, the other two Orders having a prolocutor who presides over their deliberations. Votes must be given by Orders, and a majority of each of the three Orders is essential to the passing of any measure. These synods, which are recognised in every instance by the legislature, have power to hold property with perpetual succession. They assess on the several parishes, according to their ability, contributions towards the support of the Church's work. By the combination of the voluntary principle with moderate endowments not tied up to particular churches, but generally applicable according to the varying necessities of different localities, a wise and economical system of Church finance has been worked out in the colonies, which well deserves attention. The withdrawal of subsidies from public funds—generally spoken of as dis-establishment, although very different from what we associate with the word in reference to the Church in England—has been carried out in nearly every colony. It has always been received with not unnatural alarm; but the result has not justified such apprehensions; when the first pressure has passed, it has drawn out a measure of self-help and interest in Church extension utterly unknown under the system of

Power of synods

State aid. The change has never been suddenly effected; vested and life interests have always been respected, and time has been given in which moderate endowments have been raised, not sufficient to supersede voluntary effort, but enough to encourage and supplement it.

The decennial gathering of bishops of the whole Anglican Communion at Lambeth, which now appears to be permanently established, while it claims no sort of legal authority, must have a power of binding together the widely-scattered branches of the Church which no legal authority could confer.

<small>Lambeth Conferences</small>

But when synods had been established, the Church had not acquired liberty to elect her own bishops. The choice, even though no other connection with the State remained, continued to be vested in the Crown. Liberty was acquired slowly and peaceably. In 1861 the Synod of Toronto, having constituted the see of Huron, elected a bishop, and the priest so chosen was sent to England and consecrated under letters patent. In the following year the same synod constituted the see of Ontario, and letters patent having meanwhile been discredited, the bishop was consecrated under royal mandate in Canada, the first instance of a consecration of a bishop on Canadian soil. But in 1867 a third step was taken. It being necessary to consecrate a coadjutor to the aged Bishop of Toronto, the formal application for a royal mandate was made, and the Colonial Secretary replied 'that it was not the part of the Crown to interfere in the creation of a new bishop or bishopric, and not consistent with the dignity

<small>Autonomy of the colonial churches</small>

of the Crown that he should advise Her Majesty to issue a mandate which would not be worth the paper on which it was written, and which, having been sent out to Canada, might be disregarded in the most complete manner.' Thus the election and consecration of the co-adjutor bishop began and ended with the Church, and established a precedent which has been freely followed elsewhere.

As these pages draw to a close, the magnitude of the work with which they have dealt impresses itself not less than the impossibility of doing justice to it in so small a compass. We are also driven to consider the present position, and to forecast the almost immediate future. Is the present a temptation to despair or a stimulus to greater effort, in view of positions gained and the prospects of enlarging horizons? As to the colonial churches, their position is assured; they are at least bound up with the expansion of the empire, and possibly will increase with larger growth, and will survive or escape from shocks which may arrest material progress. But in the spread of Christianity among heathen peoples, is there encouragement or the reverse? The Bishop of Durham, in a paper on the 'Comparative Progress of Ancient and Modern Missions,' declares that 'history is an excellent cordial for drooping courage.' He shows that if at the present time Christians bear to the whole human race a proportion 'a little more or a little less than one-third,' at the time of Constantine's conversion they were not more than $\frac{1}{150}$th of the whole. There were Christians in England, we know, when Tertullian wrote, before the end of the second century.

Yet when St. Augustine landed, four centuries later, he found them weak and feeble, having done nothing to convert the Teutonic invaders who had dwelt in the island for a century; and more than twenty years elapsed before the Gospel which Augustine preached in Kent passed over the borders into Sussex. The religion of Imperial Rome, interwoven with its history and the texture of its life, domestic and political, held out against the Gospel for centuries, as does Brahmanism now. For the first two hundred years of its existence, the Roman Church was Greek and Oriental rather than Latin. Its members were foreigners, who had made Rome their abiding-place: its bishops were Greek, and its language also. For some time after Constantine's conversion, the influential classes of Rome were in great part Pagan, so far as they were anything. The case of Athens was not dissimilar. St. Paul, though eminently successful with the mixed and floating population of Corinth, produced no immediate effect on the historic centre of Greek culture and religion. But the Goths and Vandals, who poured down upon the Roman empire, were evangelised rapidly and silently; and here we see a counterpart of what is going on among the aboriginal tribes of India, whose numbers are estimated at 40,000,000. Let it be further remembered that distinct missionary work was not commenced in India until 1814, and we find from the census returns that the number of Christians in India, excluding the members of the Church of Rome, was, in 1851, 1861, 1871, and 1881, 91,000, 138,000, 224,000, and 417,000 respectively, showing a steady increase of 53 per cent. in the first decade, 61 per cent. in the second decade, and 86 per cent. in the third decade.

A statistician has recently calculated that in another century the English-speaking peoples of the world will number a thousand millions; but if there be any value in the conjecture that the English language, already so popular among the educated classes in India that they feel insulted if addressed by an Englishman in their own tongue, will become general throughout Hindostan, the calculation will be seen at once to fall far below the due estimate. The prospect may well humble, and should certainly impress with a sense of responsibility every man of English birth.

<small>The spread of the English-speaking races</small>

Mr. J. R. Green, in his 'History of the English People,' has embodied the following forecast of the results of the outspread of the many branches of the English-speaking race. He writes:—

'The spirit, the influence of all these branches will remain one, and in thus remaining one, before half a century is over it will change the face of the world. As two hundred millions of Englishmen fill the valley of the Mississippi, as fifty millions assert their lordship over Australasia, their vast power will tell through Britain on the old world of Europe, whose nations will have shrunk into insignificance before it. What the issues of such a world-wide change may be, not even the wildest day-dreamer will dare to dream. But one issue is inevitable. In the centuries that lie before us the primacy of the world will be with the English people. English institutions, English speech, English thought will become the main features of the political, the social, the intellectual life of mankind.'

This prophecy, inspiriting and elevating as it is, has its spiritual application, not less encouraging. In all these lands, whither the Anglo-Saxon race drifts and settles, Christianity, imported, perhaps with all its differences and divisions, from Great Britain, will supply the people with spiritual life. It is a petty and unstatesmanlike ambition that desires that the daughter churches, which shall grow up in other lands shall be exact counterparts of their mother. The future of Christendom may well be left to the moulding of the Divine Spirit which animates it, and it is ours to believe that while many of the standards to which we cling, bearing as they do on their front the stamp of local controversies long ago composed, will find no place in the systems of younger churches, the very diversities of creed, which now separate Christians, may, in the nations which are not yet converted, find their solution in a Christianity containing all that is necessary for Catholic unity and, while bearing abundant signs of its origin, yet adapted to the thoughts and yearnings of the peoples who cling to it. Is it a wild day-dream that expects that these churches in their full maturity may exercise an overmastering influence on the churches of the old world? that the great Church of the Papacy may be led to adopt an attitude more in accordance with the needs of thoughtful men? that the great Eastern Church, with her splendid past, may emerge from her isolation and rise equal to the sublime possibilities that lie before her? that the corrupt churches, which now cling with tenacity to their traditions, but show little zeal or other sign of life—the Copts, the Armenians, the Syrians, the Nestorians—may be led to the work of self-reformation? and that the peoples which at present are no peoples, but are hastening on, under the influence of the Christian countries of Europe, to be born, as it were, in a day, may 'become the kingdoms of our Lord and of His Christ'?

INDEX.

ABBEOKUTA, 153
Aborigines, Australian, 80–83
Abraham, Bishop, 91
Acadians, persecution of, 29
Adelaide, Bishop of, 73, 77
Agra, 180
Albany Mission, 82
Alexander I. Pope, 2
Algoma, Bishopric of, 37
Alington, Rev. C. A. 147
Alms-Dish, American, 25
Amatoza tribe, 124
American Church, 19 *et seq.*
— colonies, loss of, 67
Amsterdam, New, 5
Anaiteum Island, 98, 104
Anderson, Bishop, 41
Anne, Queen, 15
Armstrong, Bishop, 121
Ascension, Isle of, 133
Athabasca, Bishopric of, 45
Atkin, Rev. J. 106
Auckland, Bishop of, 95, 109
Auer, Bishop, 156
Australia, Diocese of, 72
Australian Board of Missions, 102
— Church, growth of, 79

BACON, Lord, 7
Baker, Sir S. 148
Ballaarat, See of, 76
Baltimore, Lord, 5, 70
Banks' Islands, 104
Barbados, 4, 10, 56
Barry, Bishop, 79
Basutoland, 132
Bathurst, See of, 75
Bechuanaland, 132
Beckett, Rev. Canon, 132
Berkeley, Bishop, 21
— Lord, 5
Bickersteth, Bishop (Japan), 197
Bishoprics, list of colonial, 17
Blair, Dr. 12
Blantyre, 147
Blomfield, Bishop, 16
Bombay, 5, 177
Boone, Bishop, 192
Borneo, missions in, 197
Botany Bay, 70
Bowen, Bishop, 153
'Boyd,' H.M.S. 84
Boyle, Hon. Robert, 9, 70
— Lectureships, 9
Brahmanism, 169
Bray, Dr. 12
— Libraries, 12, 13
Brett, Rev. W. H. 61 *et seq.*
Brisbane, Bishops of, 74
Brooke, Rajah, 197
Broughton, W. G., Archdeacon and Bishop, 72, 206
Budd, Rev. H. 41

BUDDHISM

Buddhism, 169
Burmah, 177
Burton, Capt. 146, 148
— Sir W. W. 72
— Rev. Dr. 20
Butler, Bishop, 15, 54

CABOT, S. 2

Calcutta, 5
— See of, 176
Caldwell, Bishop, 186, 188
Caledonia, Bishopric of, 52
Callaway, Bishop, 125, 126
Campbell, Hon. J. 76
Canada, 5
— Dominion of, 42
— North-West, 39 et seq., 44 et seq.
Canadian Pacific Railway, 43, 52
Cape of Good Hope, 6
Carey, William, 15, 164
Carleton, Sir Guy, 30
Carolinas, 5, 11
Caulfield, Bishop, 56
Cawnpore, 177, 180
Central Africa, Bishop of, 122
— — Universities Mission to, 18
Cetewayo, chief, 130
Ceylon, 6, 183
Chaka, chief, 127
Chandra, Lala Ram, 181
Chapman, Bishop, 184
Charles I. 4
— II. 39
China, missions in, 192
— Inland Mission, 194
Chiswell, Rev. A. 138
Chota Nagpore, 178
Christian Faith Society, 10
Chimmnnm Lall, 181
Clergy Reserves (Canada), 38
Cochran, Rev. W. 40
Codrington College, 57, 58, 157
— General, 58

EAST

Codrington, Rev. R. H., 107
Coke, T. 21
Colborne, Sir J. 38
Colenso, Bishop, 121, 128
Coleridge, Bishop, 56
Coles, Rev. J. 140
Colombo, Bishop Chapman of, 135
Colonial Bishoprics Council, 17, 206
Columbia, British, 50
— Bishop of, 51
Columbus, Christopher, 2
Compton, Bishop, 12, 13
Congo River, 151
Convocation of Canterbury, 14
Cook, Captain, 69, 84, 112
Corea, the, 197
Cotterill, Bishop, 121, 125
Cotton, Bishop, 178
Cowie, Bishop, 95
Cromwell, 4
Crowther, Rev. S. afterwards Bishop, 154, 155
Cyprus, 6

DANISH Missions to India, 15

Davis, J. 113
Delaware, Lord, 8
Delhi, 177
Devil-worshippers, 186
'Dido,' H.M.S. 97
Dingaarn, chief, 127
Ditchingham Sisterhood, 53
Dodgson, Rev. E. H. 134
Domingia, 159
Douglas, Bishop, 183
Drake, Sir F. 3
Duaterra, 86
Dunedin, See of, 91
Durham, Bishop of, 211
Dutch Republic, conquests by the, 4

EAST INDIA COMPANY, 4, 5, 13

East Indies, Missions in, 160

EDINBURGH

Edinburgh, H.R.H. the Duke of, 124
Edward VI. 3
Edwardes, Sir H. 182
Edward's Island, Prince, 6
Elgin, Earl of, 196
Eliot, John, 11
Elizabeth, Queen, 3
Emma, Queen, 115
Episcopate, monarchical idea of, 207
Eugenius, Pope, 2

FALKLAND ISLANDS, 6
— — Bishop of, 66
Fallangia, 159
Farler, Archdeacon, 147
Farringia, 159
Feild, Bishop, 32
Ferguson, Bishop, 157
Ferrar, Nicholas, 8, 70
Fiji, 6, 110
Foreign Plantations, Council of, 9
French, Bishop, 180
Frere, Sir H. E. B. 142, 146, 182
Frobisher, Admiral, 3, 7, 70
Fulford, Bishop, 35

GARDINER, Captain Allen, 66
Georgia, 11
Gibraltar, 5
Gibson, Bishop of London, 21
Gilbert, Sir H. 3, 8
Gladstone, Right Hon. W. E. 207
Glass, Corporal, 133
Gobat, Bishop, 141
Goodenough, Commodore, 109
Gordon, Hon. Sir A. H. 111
— Rev. Patrick, 20
Gossner, Pastor, 179
Goulburn, See of, 75
Grafton and Armidale, See of, 74

INDIAN

Grant, Capt, 148
Gray, Bishop, 120 *et seq.* 134, 206
Green, Mr. J. R. 212
Gregory, Pope XIII. 194
— Rev. F. A. 139
Grey, Sir G. 92, 123, 134
Guiana, British, 6, 60
— Bishop of, 64

HALE, Bishop, 74, 77, 81
Hannington, Bishop, 149, 150
Harper, Bishop, 91
Hatteras Indians, 3
Hau-hau fanaticism, 94
'Havannah,' H.M.S. 100
Hawaiian Islands, 112
'Hawk,' Church-ship, 32
Hawkins, Admiral, 3
Hayti, church in, 59
'Hazard,' H.M.S. 89
Heber, Bishop, 177
Heke, John, 89
Henry VII. 2
— VIII. 2
Hobhouse, Bishop, 91
Holly, Bishop, 60
Honduras, British, 58
Hongi, chief, 86
Honolulu, Bishop of, 116
Horden, Bishop, 45
Howard, John, 69
Hubbard, Rev. A. 181
Hudson's Bay, 5
— — Company, 30, 42
Hunt, Rev. R. 8, 70
Huron, See of, 209

INDIA, languages of, 167
— missions in, 160 *et seq.*
— peoples of, 166
— religions of, 169
— religious statistics of, 190, 212
Indian bishops, position of, 172

INGLIS

Inglis, Bishop Charles, 22, 31
Isles des Los, 159

JACKSON, Port, 70
Jamaica, 5, 53
James, Bishop of Calcutta, 119, 176
— I. 4, 8
Japan, missions in, 194
Jenkins, Sir Leoline, 12
Jennings, Rev. M. E. 180
Johnson, Rev. R. 71
— Rev. W. P. 147
Jones, Bishop W. W. of Capetown, 122
Juliopolis, Archbishop of, 41

KAFFRARIA, 122, 123
Kafirs, the, 120 et seq.
— delusions of, 123
Kamehameha, King II. 114
— — III. 114
— — IV. 114
Karens, mission to, 180
Katharine, queen of Charles II. 5
Keble, Rev. J. 56
Kei River, 123, 124
Keith, Rev. G. 20
Kenebec River, 11
Kestell-Cornish, Bishop, 139
Key, Bishop, 127, 206
Kohimarama, 103
Kohlhoff, Rev. S. 185
Kôls, mission to, 179
Krapf, Dr. 141, 146
Kreli, Chief, 120
Kwamagwaza, 130

LABUAN, 6
Lahore, 180
Lambeth Conferences, 210
Lawrence, Miss, 140
 Sir H. 177
Leacock, Rev. H. J. 158
Lee, Prof. 87

MASSACHUSETTS

Lennoxville University, 37
Letters patent, disuse of, 210
Liberia, 156
Lifu, 101, 104
Lipscombe, Bishop, 56
Livingstone, D. 143, 145
Livingstonia, 147
Lloyd, Bishop, 13
Lucknow, 177

MACALLUM, Rev. A. 180
Macrorie, Bishop, 129
McDougall, Bishop, 198
Machray, Bishop, 41
McIlvaine, Bishop, 26
Mackenzie, Bishop C. F. 128, 143, 145
McKenzie, Bishop of Zululand, 130
Mackenzie River, Bishopric of, 45
Madagascar, 135
Madras, 5, 177
Magila, 147
Mai, 104
Malabar Church, 163
Malicolo, 102
Malo Island, 144
Mandalay, 183
Maori superstitions, 84
— war, 93
Map of Africa, 118
— Asia, 161
— Australia, 68
— New Zealand and Pacific Ocean, 85
— North America, 27
— South America, 54
Maré, 107
Maroons, the, 53
Marsden, Rev. S. 71, 75, 83, 84, 86, 97
Marshman, Mr. 164
Martyn, Rev. H. 117
Maryland, 4, 11, 13
Masasi, 147
Massachusetts, 4, 11

MATAKA

Mataka, King, 147
Mauritius, 6, 134
Medley, Bishop, 31
Melanesia, Bishopric of, 91, 116
Melanesian Mission, 96 *et seq.*
Melbourne, city and see of, 73, 76
Merriman, Archdeacon and Bishop, 123, 125, 126, 131
Middleton, Bishop, 86, 175
Milman, Bishop, 178, 179
Missionaries, training of, 205
Moffat, Dr. 132
Mohammedanism, 170
Mohawks (Indian tribe), 23
Mombasa, 141–143
Montreal, See of, 35
Moore, Bishop, 13
Moorhouse, Bishop, 76
Moosonee, Bishopric of, 44
Moravians, the, 15, 119
Morumbala, 144
Mota, 104
Mountain, Bishop Jacob, 31, 33
— Bishop G. J. 35, 41
Mpapwa, 149
Mtesa, King, 148–150
Mwembe, 147
'Myrmidon,' H.M.S. 158

NATAL, 6
— colony of, 127
Negro Education Fund, 55
Nelson, See of, 91
Neutral French, 28
New Caledonia, 101
Newcastle, Bishop of, 73, 102
New England, 4, 11
— — Company, 8
Newfoundland, 5, 31 *et seq.*
New Guinea, 83
New Holland, discovery of, 69
New Jersey, 11
New Westminster, Bishopric of, 52
New York, 5

PRETORIA

New Zealand, 6
— — See of, 73
Niger River, 153, 155
Nixon, Bishop, 119
Nobbs, Edwin, 105
Norfolk Island 103 *et seq.*
North Borneo Company, 199
North Queensland, See of, 78
Nova Scotia, 4, 5, 27 *et seq.*
— — Bishopric of, 30
Nukapu Island, 106, 109, 110
Nyanza Lakes, 143, 148

ONEIDAS (Indian tribe), 23
Onitsha, 155
Ontario, church in province of, 35
— See of, 209
Orange Free State, 131

PADDON, Capt. 98
Panda, King, 128, 130
Paramatta, 83
Paris, treaty of (1814), 6
Parkes, Sir H. 197
Palmas, Cape, 24, 156
Patrick, Bishop, 13
Patteson, Rev. J. C. (afterwards Bishop), 91, 103 *et seq.*
Payne, Bishop, 156
Penang, 177
Penick, Bishop, 157
Penn, 115
Pennsylvania, 5, 11
Perry, Bishop, 76
Perth, See of, 77
Philadelphia, Trinity Church, 23
Pinder, Rev. J. H. 59
Pitt, Rt. Hon. W. 113
Pocahontas, 8
Pongas Mission, 157
Poole, Bishop, 196
Poonindic, 81
Portugal and its conquests, 3
Pretoria, Bishop of, 132

PRIDEAUX

Prideaux, Dean, 13
Provoost, Bishop, 23

Qu'Appelle, Bishop of, 45
Quebec, See of, 31
— population of, 34

Radama I. II. III. Kings, 135, 136
Raffles, Sir S. 200
Raleigh, Sir W. 8, 60, 70
Ranavalona, Queen, 136
Rangoon, Bishop of, 180
Rawle, Bishop, 57, 157
Rebmann, Dr. 142, 146
Regina, 44
Riverina, See of, 76
'Rosario,' H.M.S. 109
Rota (Maori deacon), 90
Rotuma Island, 97
Rupert, Prince, 5
Rupert's Land, 5, 39, 41
Russia Company, 3

Saccibarbi or Cornelius, 62
Saint Helena, 5, 122, 133
St. John's, Diocese of, 122
Sandilli, Chief, 120
Sandwich, Earl of, 112
— Islands, 112
Sandys, E. 8
Santa Cruz, 105, 109
Sarawia, Rev. G. 105
Sargent, Bishop, 188
Schereschewsky, Bishop, 193
Schwartz, F. C. 164, 176, 185
Scotland, Free Kirk of, 147
— Established Church of, 147
Seabury, Bishop, 18, 22, 25
Selkirk, Earl of, 40
Selwyn, Bishop, 25, 74, 88, 97 et seq., 206
— Bishop J. R. 108 et seq.
Sharpe, Archbishop, 13
— Granville, 152
Sierra Leone, 6, 151
Singapore, 6, 200

TAPU

Six-Nation Confederacy, 23
Skelton, Rev. T. 181
Slavery, first mention of, 21
Smith, Lieut. Shergold, 149
— Sir Harry, 120
Smythies, Bishop, 148
Society for Promoting Christian Knowledge, 13, 14, 164
— for the Propagation of the Gospel in Foreign Parts, 14, 20, 138, 164
— South American, 18, 66
— Wesleyan Missionary, the, 15, 98
— Baptist Missionary, the, 15
— London Missionary, the, 16, 98, 103, 114, 136, 138, 148, 193
— Church Missionary, the, 16, 40, 138, 148, 152, 154
— Colonial and Continental, the, 17
Solomon Islands, 103
Soudan, the, 151
'Southern Cross,' mission ship, 109
Southey's 'Life of Wesley,' 20
Spain and its Conquests, 4
Speke, Capt. 148
Spencer, Bishop A. G. 32
Stanley, H. M. 148, 149, 151
Stanton, Bishop, 78
Statistics of missionary contributions, 203
Steere, Bishop, 146, 147
Stewart, Bishop, 34
Still, Rev. J. 108
Strachan, Bishop (Toronto) 37,
— (Rangoon), 206
Straits Settlements, 200
Sydney, city of, 71
— See of, 75
Synge, Rev. E. 75
Synods, 206 et seq.

Tamahana Wiremu, 91, 92
Tanganyika, Lake, 148
Tapu, system of, 86, 113

TASMANIA

Tasmania, See of, 73
— Bishop of, 78
Tenison, Archbishop, 13, 14
Thaba 'Nchu, 132
Theebaw, King, 183.
Tippahee, chief, 84
Titcomb, Bishop, 180
Toronto, University at, 37
Toungloo, 178
Townsend, Rev. H. 154, 155
Tozer, Bishop, 145
Tranquebar, Danish Mission at, 15
Trinidad, 6, 57
Tristan d'Acunha, 133
Tufnell, Bishop, 74
Tugela River, 130
— Turner, Bishop of Calcutta, 119, 176
Tuttle, Bishop, 24
Tutty, Rev. W. 28

UMTATA RIVER, 126
Umhala, Chief, 120
'Undine' yacht, 100
Universities and colleges, colonial, 204
Utrecht, treaty of, 5

VANCOUVER, Captain, 112
'Venn, Henry,' steamer, 156
Vidal, Bishop, 153
Virginia, 3, 4
— Company, 8
Volkner, Rev. C. S. 94

WADROKAL, Rev. 109
Wairau, outbreak at, 89
Waitangi, treaty of, 6
Waitara, 93
Wales, New South, 6
Warangesda, 82
Waters, Archdeacon, 124
Weeks, Bishop, 153, 158
Wellesley, Lord, 164

ZULULAND

Wellington, first Duke of, 72
— See of, 91
Wesley, Rev. J. 20, 21, 97
— Rev. C. 20
West, Rev. J. 40
— Africa Mission, 59
— Indian Church, 53 *et seq.*
— — — Society, 157
Western Australia or Perth, See of, 77
Whanganui, conference at, 90
Whipple, Bishop, 24
Whitaker, Mr., 8
White, Bishop, 23
Wilberforce, Bishop, 116
'Wild North Land,' author of the, 47
Wilkinson, Lewis, 158
Williams, Bishop (China and Japan), 193
— Rev. H. and W. 87
Wilson, Bishop, 21
— — Daniel, 119, 177
Windsor, N.S., King's College, 31
Windward Islands, Diocese of, 57
Winnipeg, 40, 42
Winter, Rev. R. R. 181
Wolseley, Sir G. 43
Woodfall, Master, 7, 70
'Wright, Henry,' steamer, 150

XAVIER, ST. FRANCIS, 164, 195

YOUNG, FISHER, 105
— J. 113
York, Duke of, 5
Yoruba, 153

ZAMBESI RIVER, 144–146
Zanzibar, 141
Zenanas, work in, 190
Ziegenbalg, 163, 185
Zululand, Bishopric of, 130

www.ingramcontent.com/pod-product-compliance
Lightning Source LLC
Chambersburg PA
CBHW021802230426
43669CB00008B/606